JOB
U

JOB

U

HOW TO FIND WEALTH AND SUCCESS

BY DEVELOPING THE SKILLS

COMPANIES ACTUALLY NEED

Nicholas Wyman

CROWN
BUSINESS

New York

Crown Business books are available at special discounts for bulk
purchases for sales promotions or corporate use. Special editions,
including personalized covers, excerpts of existing books, or books with
corporate logos, can be created in large quantities for special needs. For
more information, contact Premium Sales at (212) 572-2232 or e-mail
specialmarkets@randomhouse.com.

Library of Congress Cataloging-in-Publication Data is available upon
request.

ISBN 978-0-8041-4078-2
eBook ISBN 978-0-8041-4079-9

Printed in the United States of America

Cover design by Jess Morphew
Cover illustration: Andrew Gibbs
Cover background photograph: Grzym/Shutterstock
Author photograph: DouglasGorenstein.com

10 9 8 7 6 5 4 3 2 1

First Edition

Contents

JOB

Prologue

This book aims to change the entire conversation about what the right path to a rewarding and prosperous career can look like: the conversation going on at company headquarters, in college admissions offices, and around kitchen tables across the nation. It will shatter the false dogma that college is the best—or only—path for every ambitious young person, and it will provide the spark for a jobs revolution by offering a new and different way of looking at the path to a fulfilling and successful work life.

Whether you are right out of high school, a recent college graduate, or well along in your career journey, you'll discover affordable and accessible pathways to a respected, rewarding, and well-paid career. Indeed, by the time you finish this book, you will have a whole new outlook and road map for how to find the best way to add value—and be valued—in today's job market.

The fact is, it doesn't matter how young or old you are, what field you work in or aspire to work in, or what your background looks like. Today we are all facing the reality that unemployment and *under*employment are at record highs—across all regions of the country, across all industries, and across all income and educational levels. Yet, at the same time, millions of jobs are being left vacant—or, worse, being sent overseas because there are not enough U.S. workers with the skills to do them or do them well.

Here are the hard facts. Today around thirteen million Americans, some with college degrees, are unemployed, and that does not include those who are *under*employed or have given up trying to find work. Yet three million positions remain unfilled, and a quarter of American businesses say they have trouble finding people with the practical, technical, job-ready skills they need. In the manufacturing industry, a sector that has long been the lynchpin of our economy, it's even worse. Companies report six hundred thousand unfilled manufacturing jobs. Thus, companies are struggling to find enough skilled people to justify moving jobs back to America.

In short, there are millions of willing people waiting on the sidelines, yet not enough of them have the practical skills required to keep companies staffed and the economy humming. One reason for this supply-demand imbalance—known as the job-skills, or middle-skills, gap—is simply that too many job seekers, including many of today's college graduates, are finishing their educations without practical work experience or the soft skills needed to land a job: the skills to be part of and work on a team and navigate the day-to-day rigors of a modern workplace. For reasons outlined in the coming chapters, today many young people are graduating from college with a solid footing in liberal arts subjects—such as art history and sociology and literature—but little to no exposure to or training in the technical and practical skills that so many of today's jobs and companies actually require. This skills gap has major ramifications not only for individual job seekers and companies but for the economy at large—particularly as more baby boomers retire, more "knowledge jobs" become automated, and more manufacturing work returns to the United States from overseas.

The good news is that the same middle-skills gap that frustrates thousands of employers represents an opportunity for every person who is deciding what to do with the rest of his or her life, and for every college grad who cannot find a good-paying job. It represents opportunity for every seasoned worker whose livelihood is threatened by automation and outsourcing; for every midlife career changer or laid-off worker for whom a new job will necessarily require new skills; for every man or woman looking to rejoin the workforce after a lengthy absence or maternity leave; for all the parents who can't afford to spend hundreds of thousands of dollars on their kids' education, and for every parent who *can* pay those bills but asks, "Is this the best investment I can make in my child's future?" And it represents opportunity for every executive, manager, or other professional who has reached a point in life where they crave satisfaction through tangible, hands-on work; for anyone at any stage in their career seeking what Matthew Crawford describes in *Shop Class as Soulcraft* as "the satisfactions of manifesting oneself concretely in the world through manual competence."[1]

But the doors to these opportunities can't be found at traditional elite colleges. Nor can they be found at any of the hundreds of second- or third-tier colleges or universities—schools that carry similar high price tags but don't confer the same prestige and connections on their graduates when they enter the job market.

In fact, the paths to these opportunities can be found only *outside* traditional four-year universities, in the burgeoning opportunities of skills-based education, such as those found through vocational training courses, technical schools, community colleges, apprenticeship programs, and more. In other words, in the educational pathways that equip smart, ambitious students with *the job-ready skills that companies actually need.*

Please note that I'm not talking here about pathways to minimum-wage, dead-end, or revolving-door jobs that no one wants to do. I'm talking about the skills-based learning opportunities that lead to well-paying, respectable careers as electricians, master chefs, cardiovascular technologists, machinists, aircraft mechanics, auto technicians, dental hygienists, welders, mechatronics engineers, and air ambulance paramedics, to name just a few. When I talk about people with skills-based careers, I'm not talking about low-paid, "old style" factory workers; I'm talking about the highly skilled and well-compensated technicians repairing the engines at Boeing that enable millions of passengers to fly each day, or building the complex gas turbine generators for Siemens that power communities around the world, or installing the cutting-edge robotic assembly machines at Volkswagen—one of the largest automotive manufacturers in the world. I'm talking about the entrepreneurs who run their own photography studios, the artisans who fill their days hand-crafting high-end furniture, and the apprentice chefs preparing meals at your favorite neighborhood bars and restaurants. I'm talking about the people who build our homes and bridges, monitor our health, care for our sick and diseased, and keep our complex IT networks running; the people who keep our new world of "advanced manufacturing" humming by programming and operating our computer-controlled tools and robots; the people we need and call (and pay a hefty sum to) when our pipes spring a leak or our furnaces go kaput on a frosty winter night. These are the men and women who form the backbone of our economy and society. And almost all of them learned their skills through high school vocational education, two-year associate degree programs, traineeships or apprenticeships, formal and informal company-based training, or one of the other alternatives to traditional college you'll read about in this book. Contrary to popular belief, a surprising percentage of them earn more than their peers who spent four years and tens of thousands of dollars earning baccalaureate degrees—a fact lost on too many parents and guidance counselors who think that the traditional college/university track is the best or only pathway to building a prosperous career.

We have all been sold on the notion that college is for everyone and have been promised that a traditional four-year degree is a guaranteed ticket to a well-paid, secure professional future. But the truth is, college has never been for everyone, and today, more often than not, it doesn't deliver on that promise. According to new research from the Federal Reserve Bank of New York reported in the *New York Times,* the jobless rate for college graduates under age twenty-five averaged 8.2 percent in 2013 (compared to 5.4 percent in 2007), and the underemployment rate for college graduates ages twenty-two to twenty-seven was a woeful 44 percent—clear evidence that, as the *Times* editorial board concluded, "a college education, in and of itself, does not create good jobs at good pay."[2]

And let's not forget that a four-year degree comes at a hefty cost; the dark side of college education, of course, is student loan debt, which in the United States has recently surpassed *$1 trillion,* the second largest category of personal debt, just behind property mortgages. In fact, at the time of this writing, Americans collectively owe more in student loan debt than the entire nation owes on credit card debt. Think of that. Americans collectively owe $1 trillion on student loans. And let's remember 40 percent who start a four-year college degree have failed to complete the BA after six years.

The assumption that every student should receive a

college education becomes more outrageous when you consider the fact that people possess a huge range of different intelligences, skill sets, and interests—some people just don't thrive in a traditional classroom but are masters when working with their hands. For some, the dream career may indeed be found in the halls of a law firm or corporate headquarters or investment bank, but for every one of these people there exists another equally intelligent individual who is just as passionate about building airplanes, tinkering with robotics, or restoring antique furniture. And while there is certainly nothing wrong with harboring lofty ambitions to save lives as a doctor or surgeon or cancer researcher, is it any less noble to dream of making a difference in the world as an emergency medical technician, or home health care aid, or a social entrepreneur? We all have different passions, talents, and ambitions. So why are we asked to follow the same educational paths? The answer isn't lack of opportunities; it's lack of information.

Why is the existence of countless accessible, affordable alternatives to traditional higher education such a well-kept secret? Why is it that a high school senior, upon entering her college counselor's office, will be asked her SAT scores and grade point average, then presented with a stack of brochures for four-year colleges she may have an unrealistic chance of getting into, with no mention of the fact that other (far less expensive) options exist? Why is it that high schools across the nation are scaling back or closing their vocational courses or programs—to the point where only a small number still even offer the traditional "shop class"? Why is it that, as much as we mythologize the ideal of American entrepreneurship and laud American advances in technological innovation, our secondary educational system is still woefully slow— lagging behind virtually all other developed nations—to integrate computer science, engineering, and other technical competencies into their core curricula?

Why is there still a lingering stigma against vocational and technical learning? Why do parents still announce their child's plans to attend a polytechnic institute or community college any less loudly and proudly than they would boast of their child's acceptance to a third- or fourth-tier college (let alone an elite one)? This book doesn't promise to hold the answers to all these questions. But it does promise to show you how you (or your child, if you are a parent) can avoid falling prey to these misconceptions.

My own career offers an example of how the development of a marketable skill through a nontraditional education can set a young person on a rewarding and successful pathway through life.

Conventional wisdom tells us that the way to succeed is to follow our passions. That was certainly true in my case. Yet my pursuit was almost nipped in the bud by my well-meaning parents, who had other plans for young Nick. They had sent me to an exclusive high school with the expectation I would go on to college. My father was a university professor, and it seemed natural that his son would earn a bachelor's degree at a minimum. The adults around me told me that college was the logical choice. My peers thought I was crazy to pass up all the "social opportunities" that college had to offer. But my happiest memories were not of books and classrooms but of cooking at my grandmother's side, soaking up the glorious smells of her kitchen. I knew in my heart that college was not where I belonged at that point in my life.

Being a psychologist, and a clever parent to boot, my father realized that logic alone would not dissuade me. So he turned to a time-tested parental tool for getting children to toe the line: subterfuge. The next thing I knew, my father had arranged for me to work in a local kitchen whose uninspired, tasteless dishes, he figured, would surely break my heart. I still remember the worn patch on the tile floor where the chef had stood for the past twenty years melting slices of cheese on the slabs of dreaded meat he passed off as chicken parmigiana. Would this be my lot in life?

My father's ploy worked. Within a few weeks I was ready to abandon the cooking life and march off to college. I still remember his chuckle as I told him: "Gee, Dad, you were right. Being a chef is not for me." Luckily, a friend convinced me to hang on to my dream, and helped me land a culinary apprenticeship in an outstanding international hotel kitchen in my hometown of Melbourne, Australia—a kitchen where something as simple as chicken stock was created with loving care.

Then, as now, new apprentices were assigned the

unglamorous chores of the trade, and I got plenty of them: chopping lettuce; peeling onions, garlic, and bag after bag of potatoes; and cleaning up after the head chef. It was hard work. I was on my feet twelve hours a day, and during serving hours our kitchen staff moved at warp speed. But I loved it because I was learning (and applying) new skills every day. And I was doing something for which I had an unquenchable passion: cooking.

In the end, that four-year apprenticeship was more fulfilling and rewarding than any traditional classroom experience could have been. Three years into it, I was named captain of the Australian youth culinary team, which won gold in the 1988 Culinary Olympics held in Frankfurt, Germany. I'll never forget the blood, sweat, and tears that went into serving 115 portions of our award-winning Desert Bloom, an Australian rabbit dish—victory made all the sweeter because the fifty pounds of rabbit meat we'd brought with us from Australia had been held up in German customs. Fortunately, problem solving is one of the many "soft skills" you learn as a chef apprentice, and we were able to prevail because within twenty-four hours (time management), the four of us (team building) had found (initiative) a local source of rabbit meat, prepared our dish, and outscored twenty other national teams. Chalk one up for the Aussies!

As I became more skilled, more career opportunities presented themselves. The next year I was named Australian apprentice of the year and received a scholarship to study and work in some of the best kitchens in Europe. These included the Gleneagles Hotel in Scotland, London's Claridge's hotel, and others, where I had the life-changing experience of serving the queen; Prince Charles and Diana, princess of Wales; King Constantine of Greece, and other royalty.

My London experience even included a stint at the Ritz, where high tea is an art. It was there that I was introduced to a side of the restaurant business with which I had little experience: buying and selling at the markets. In the early hours, when few Londoners were stirring, the city's food markets were bustling. Fresh fish, meat, poultry, and vegetables traded at a furious rate. Those predawn forays into the food markets opened my eyes to an unseen slice of London culture and to a work experience that no traditional classroom could have imparted.

Yet my stint as a chef did not close the door to academic learning or other possibilities, as my parents had feared. After several years of striving to perfect the art of cookery, I was satisfied with my career but looking for more. If working in those storied kitchens had taught me anything, it was that being a good chef involved more than good cooking. I needed to also learn about marketing, customer relations, managing people, and running a business. So I went back to school, eventually completing a master's of business administration. At first I had feared the years spent out of school would put me behind, or at a disadvantage, compared to my conventionally educated peers, but in fact, the self-confidence and problem-solving abilities I developed through my apprenticeship and work experience served me well during those years. I've since continued with executive education at Harvard Business School and the Hauser Center at the Harvard Kennedy School, and today, as CEO of the Institute for Workplace Skills and Innovation, I have the privilege of helping hundreds of young people do exactly as I did—develop respected and well-paid careers via journeys other than the traditional high-school-to-college route.

You'll meet many of these young people in the chapters that follow, including a mechanic on the world car-racing circuit; a photographer who serves New York City's theater and media community; a young apprentice who is helping to build six-hundred-ton electric generators; young English lads who spend each day restoring one of World War II's most iconic aircraft—the RAF Spitfire—and countless other individuals who nabbed "dream jobs" you may have never even heard of by following nontraditional paths. Through their stories, you'll learn why we have so many people without jobs and jobs without people. You'll come to understand how society's myopic focus on "college for everyone" may be hurting as many young people as it helps, and you will see why the antidote to this misconception is to embrace the alternate routes to attractive occupations that do not require a traditional four-year college education.

You'll read about these pathways that do not necessarily require a four-year college education (or the resulting mountains of student debt), such as apprenticeships, occupational certificate programs, associate degrees, on-the-job skills training—and how to find, choose, and pursue the path best suited to your passions, goals, and abilities. And, most important, you'll learn how to parlay that education into the most fulfilling and best-paying dream job in any field.

I have one of those dream jobs myself—helping young people make the difficult transition between school and the workplace. At any given time, the organization I'm privileged to represent has six hundred to seven hundred young men and women in mentored apprenticeship and trainee programs—learning and earning as they develop skills that employers badly need. If our past record holds up, 82 percent of these people will complete their three- or four-year programs and receive a certification in trade specialties. More than ten thousand people have followed this very path. Upon completing their apprenticeships each gets a nice pay increase and the opportunity to continue working for the same company that sponsored their training. No frantic job search. No education loans to pay off. And most will advance over time to positions with greater responsibility and still better pay. Some will eventually become managers or owners of the companies that had the foresight to invest in their training. As an executive of a billion-dollar advanced manufacturing facility told me, "Someday these people will be running our plant."

This work has taken me to the United Kingdom, Europe, Southeast Asia, and the United States, where I see the same problems: vocational educational programs that are disrespected and in decline; parents and policy makers who see a college/university education as *the only sure* pathway for young people; and a middle-skills gap that is hamstringing economic progress, particularly in the sciences, technology, and manufacturing. On the brighter side, I've also encountered companies, educators, and policy makers who are attacking these problems with unique strategies and close collaboration. Some are German companies that are exporting and creating hybrids of their centuries-old tradition of apprenticeship training. Others are communities reinventing education through partnerships between multinational corporations and local school districts. You'll meet many of these pioneers in the pages that follow.

Whether you are a high school student (or the parent of a high school student) trying to figure out how you are going to shoulder the heavy burden of college tuition (or trying to decide whether you even want to go to college!), or one of the two million college students graduating into one of the most competitive job markets in decades (and carrying the average student loan debt of $29,400), or someone well along in your career journey, know that a multitude of options for acquiring valuable, marketable skills that will open the door to greater employment opportunities *do* exist. And know that the door to the opportunities you seek may well be found in one of the nontraditional pathways you'll read about in this book.

The paths described here—apprenticeships, vocational and technical education, certification programs, associate degrees, and on-the-job skills training—are the solution to a large slice of our unemployment and underemployment problems. They are the solution for employers who can't find skilled people, *and* for job seekers who want to become more employable and job-ready in an increasingly competitive economy. Through my work I am in a unique position to see why we need united, decisive action now, not only to save the younger generation from chronic unemployment and resuscitate our middle class, but for the future of our global economy. And there is no time like the present. Some may say change has already overtaken us, and that we are too late to overturn the known "college for everyone" model or to prevent the next generation of unskilled workers from being replaced by technology and automation and relegated to the unemployment lines. Yet new research coming out of prestigious economic institutions and think tanks—much of which will be unveiled for the first time in these pages—tells us otherwise.

It's time to get moving on these proven pathways. A jobs revolution is already upon us. To ensure a more prosperous future for ourselves, our children, and generations to come, we need to throw out models that no longer work. We must abandon old assumptions and embrace a new way of thinking about what a successful educational and career path can look like. All it takes is a shift in thinking and the courage to act. In doing so we can give millions of people the purpose, direction, and fulfillment that comes from satisfying, respected, and well-paid work.

1

People Without Jobs and Jobs Without People

I meet lots of interesting people in my line of work. Too many have graduated from high school with no marketable skills or experience and no idea of what to do next. They drift from one low-paid job to another, never feeling that they've found their place or their calling. "I was doing one thing for one month and nothing for the next," nineteen-year-old Christopher told me. "I felt lost, unsure of where to go next." Others are college graduates, like Michelle, who despite their expensive degrees and often after several false starts, still can't seem to find fulfilling and meaningful work. Still others are more seasoned workers with plenty of experience under their belts who are suddenly finding themselves displaced by automation, outsourcing, or life circumstances that caused them to leave the workforce temporarily—only to find their jobs are gone upon their return.

Does this sound familiar? Do you know anyone who is feeling lost, without the skills, qualifications, or a plan for landing a rewarding and well-paying job? We meet people like this of all ages and in all classes of society, though it's often those from disadvantaged backgrounds who have the most trouble negotiating the transition into their working lives—not because they are any less talented or intelligent, but simply because they don't have a financial safety net to fall back on, or the community connections and support networks to help find their first job. Their parents may not have a friend or business owner they can call on for a favor—"My child is looking for work at the moment. Could you help them?" And the majority simply haven't had access to the kind of information, education, and resources they need to navigate the complex and hypercompetitive twenty-first-century workforce.

And many are young—the members of the rising generation upon whom we have placed all our hopes of promise and progress. Jennifer Silva, a researcher on young adults and the author of the book *Coming Up Short*,[1] has documented the uncertainty and instability felt by American eighteen- to thirty-four-year-olds struggling to get a toehold in today's world of work. It's not a pretty picture. Many find themselves moving back in with their parents, simply because they cannot afford not to. Some struggle to earn college degrees while racking up overwhelming loans. Others are forced to resort to short-term or minimum-wage jobs in order to pay back those loans for an education that bought them next to nothing. Some join the military hoping to take advantage of its education benefits, yet sadly are unable to find employment upon returning from serving their country.

And way too many of our young adults today get trapped in the never-ending cycle of debt and dependence that leaves them doubting or giving up hope they will ever be able to have the successful and rewarding work life we all dream of achieving.

Silva's subjects are of "a family and a country that has run full circle, from middle-class suburban dreams . . . back to economic insecurity, riskiness, and recession." Unable to achieve solid, decent-paying employment, the people caught in this downward spiral postpone or miss out entirely on the life events that most of us value and plan for: marriage and children, home ownership, mind-expanding travel for themselves and their children. Lacking good counseling, they make poor life and educational choices. And with no solid footholds in the present, they cannot plan for the future. Silva sees these patterns even in her own extended working-class family, writing that "my generation is slowly losing the stability hard-won by their grandparents and parents."

While things are hard for the millions of young people entering the workforce for the first time in the toughest economy in decades, the leap into the world of work must seem even more impossible for many long-term unemployed. Getting a job after a prolonged period of unemployment can be so challenging that nearly 20 percent of them—around forty million—have simply given up and withdrawn from the labor market, according to a recent Global Employment Trends report. This is particularly true for those who left school around the time of the global financial crisis, when hiring activity froze up. There were simply no openings for them. And the longer they remained unemployed, the more disengaged they became, and the harder it got for them to break the cycle, build a résumé, get a job, acquire some skills, and move up the career ladder. Many studies have shown that hiring managers are biased against the long-term unemployed job applicant, thinking, "He must lack ability" or "She must not be motivated." These assumptions and sometimes mean-spirited comments don't help those who want to work—particularly those who are out there every day, pounding the pavement, looking for work, but finding their search futile, *because they simply don't have the skills that companies are looking for.* And with each day that passes, the situation gets even worse; while some of their contemporaries are going to work every day, learning new things, moving ahead, and planning ahead, they are falling further and further behind. And the further behind they fall, the more quickly they give up hope. Both of which reduce the probability they will *ever* get onto a long-term job track and enjoy the benefits of economic security that we all want: savings in the bank, work that matters, a strong family, and a purpose-driven and meaningful life.

Making matters worse is the fact that many people entering today's workforce—whether for the first time or after a hiatus—lack not only practical skills but what I describe as "foundation," or "soft skills": skills a job seeker needs to engage successfully in the world of work and, more broadly, in life, such as problem solving, the ability to work as a member of a team, and an understanding of the evolving forms of communication in the digital age.

There is no question that young people are facing the brunt of these challenging economic times. And this makes the consequences for the future much more bleak. If we don't find a way to put these young people back on the path to gainful employment there's the potential for an entire lost generation of people who are neither in school nor in the workforce simply "getting by" by leaning on small "paychecks" provided by parents or government support. Such a scenario would not only be devastating to society, it would threaten to derail generations of economic progress.

Of course, unemployment and underemployment are not just an American problem. Across the globe, in Europe, Asia, South America, the Middle East, and elsewhere, job seekers of all races and religions are dealing with the same challenges. The politicians and business leaders in the communities in which we live all realize that a gainful and productive workforce is the key to tomorrow's economic future. And yet the percentage of unemployed young people in many parts of the Western world is stratospheric—in most cases twice the general rate of overall unemployment.

My home country of Australia, for example, is a land abundant in underground natural resources: iron ore, coal, diamonds, gold, and oil and gas. It's so flush with natural resources that historically it's been referred to as "the Lucky Country." However, though Australia enjoyed a booming economy and relatively low unemployment for an uninterrupted decade, the global financial crisis wiped out a quarter of a million jobs down under, causing unemployment among young Aussies to skyrocket to about 20 percent nationally and over 50 percent in some urban areas—and forcing the nation's leaders to come to terms with the fact that, for its luck to continue, the nation must not only develop these mineral and energy resources, it must also develop its most valuable resource of all: its human capital.

Countries in all regions of the world face economic pressure. They all seek to reduce unemployment and increase workforce participation. It makes sense. What country would not like more people contributing to the economy? What government wouldn't want more taxpayers? And what society wouldn't want to spend less on welfare and social services? Yet in a globalized world where economies are unstable, industries are being constantly upended and disrupted, and technology is developing faster than most of our skills for utilizing it, we all face the challenge of how to engage the next generation of workers.

The irony is that while millions of people are suffering from the costs of high unemployment and the disaffection and frustration that come from the inability to find a job, millions of jobs remain vacant because businesses can't find enough people with the *right* skills to do those jobs. In fact, employment studies report that more than three million U.S. job openings are unfilled, mainly due to a shortage of skilled workers. Harvard Business School professor Rosabeth Moss Kanter has calculated that as many as a third of the jobs lost during the economic turmoil that followed the 2008 meltdown reflect a mismatch between the skills employers need and those that workers actually possess.[2] As one frustrated executive in Texas put it to me simply, "Nick, we just can't find enough people with the skills we need." In my meetings with managers and executives across the globe for the purpose of researching this book, that's the one sentiment I heard again and again. And I'm far from the only one hearing it. The moderator of one conference of U.S. optical industry executives, for example, echoed my experience exactly when he told me "I couldn't get [the executives] to stop talking about the workforce shortage, which all agreed was their greatest impediment to growth." And again this is not just an American problem; more than half of Australia's corporate directors recently surveyed identified a shortage of skilled labor as their greatest economic challenge. In short, we are becoming a world of people without jobs *and* jobs without people.

Even in the manufacturing industry, which has shed positions due to outsourcing to Asia, U.S. companies are reporting they would be willing to bring these jobs back from overseas—if only they could find enough skilled people to do the work they need. Deloitte Consulting LLP and the Manufacturing Institute, a trade group, reported in 2011 that more than 80 percent of manufacturers were unable to find enough skilled talent, leaving more than six hundred thousand jobs unfilled.[3] And the areas of greatest reported shortage were in middle-skilled categories: machinists, technicians, operators, and craft positions that pay solid middle-class wages with benefits! This results not only in missed opportunities for half a million job seekers, but huge financial losses for the companies (and by extension the economy at large) as well, given that according to survey respondents, those were the positions that had the *greatest positive impact* on operational performance. As the report put it, "The workforce segments that are hardest to fill are those that impact operations the most and require the most training. From machinists and craft workers to industrial engineers and planners, the talent crunch in these critical areas is taking its toll on manufacturers' ability to meet current operation objectives and achieve longer-term strategic goals."[4]

Think about that: Millions of people want to work, yet there are not enough qualified skilled people to fill many of business's most critical positions! Conversations about how to integrate more people into the workforce and on the future of the middle class are occurring daily, yet we cannot seem to find ways to equip people with the skills to command and earn middle-class incomes. And while the global economy is still struggling to recover from the 2008 economic meltdown, companies are losing more footing and even more profits to the inability to find job-ready workers. In one study by Deloitte and the Manufacturers Institute, respondents pointed to a highly skilled, flexible workforce as "the most important factor in their effectiveness, ranking above factors such as new product innovation and increased market share." And in this they are not alone. The stakes couldn't be higher, and yet we are still currently not developing enough of the vital human capital we need to keep our companies humming.

As bad as the skills gap is today, many feel it could get worse in the years ahead as baby boomers retire, taking their experience and technical know-how with them. The workforce situation facing aerospace companies in the state of Washington provides a preview of the more general challenge. Washington's aerospace industry employs more than eighty-four thousand people. Many of these workers are already eligible for retirement, and many more are fast approaching eligibility. When company executives look around their production facilities they wonder where the next generation of machinists, welders, electricians, and other skilled employees will come from. They certainly aren't in the pipeline today. Who will step up to take their places?

A big part of the problem is that we are looking to the wrong institutions to develop and train these workers. Contrary to what most people believe, a shortage of *college-educated* workers—particularly scientists and engineers—accounts for only part of the workplace skill gap. In fact, most of the positions that remain unfilled— and that offer meaningful, rewarding, and well-paid work for many of today's unemployed now and in the future—do *not* require a college degree. Most, in fact, are jobs that can be filled by men and women with "high school–plus" education—a high school diploma *plus* an associate degree, a vocational apprenticeship, or a training certification. The research shows that while eight of the ten *fastest-growing* U.S. job categories require a college degree or better, 61 percent of *all jobs* do not. And this trend is only accelerating. Looking out to the future, only 27 percent of new jobs forecast by the Labor Department to be generated between 2014–2024, will require a college degree,[5] and data shows that by 2018, open positions requiring only on-the-job training, an associate degree, or an apprentice's certificate will hugely eclipse the openings that require advanced degrees. And according to the U.S. Bureau of Labor Statistics and reported in the *New York Times* and *Time* magazine, of the twenty occupations expected to add the most new jobs from 2012 to 2022, only one—general and operations management—requires a bachelor's degree. Middle-skills jobs with a technology bent will increase by 18 percent from 2012 to 2022.[6]

The good news is that the challenge faced by employers represents an opportunity for students and workers who embrace a skilled career path. And make no mistake: Despite what the "college for everyone" dogmatists would have you believe, these are not low-paying or low-status positions. Many—such as cardiovascular engineering technician, robotics machinist, or dental hygienist—start at upward of $50,000 a year, with many opportunities for advancement.

Even at Google, widely regarded as one of the nation's most desirable employers, a college degree is not necessarily a requirement for employment. According to Lazlo Bock, the senior vice president of people operations (a twenty-first-century term for human resources) at Google, an increasing percentage of Google's new hires have not, in fact, graduated college. When evaluating candidates, instead of a high GPA or fancy diploma, Google looks for practical expertise, problem-solving ability, humility, a desire to lead, and the willingness to learn[7]—all qualities, as you'll see throughout this book, best attained through a nontraditional, skills-based education.

There is also a popular misconception that when the economy falters, skills-based jobs are the first to go, but, in reality, middle-skills jobs are more secure than most, as geography insulates many if not most from offshore competition. Think of it this way: A big North American telecom company can pay English-speaking techies in India or the Philippines to handle customers' Internet problems over the phone or online. But what can it do when the air-conditioning in its Atlanta headquarters building goes down on a hot summer day? Nor can workers in other countries repair your car, cook you a fine meal at a local restaurant, administer the echocardiogram your doctor ordered, fix your leaking faucets or install a solar electrical system in your new house, or provide physical therapy for your injured shoulder. In many respects, middle-skills careers are more stable than most others.

Given this wealth of opportunity, why are so many

young adults still leaving school with neither marketable nor practical skills? The lingering social stigma against vocational education is not entirely to blame. Ironically, many companies are actually sabotaging their own prospects for a productive workforce by adopting a "find not build" approach to its human capital. In an attempt to reduce costs, the entry-level on-the-job training programs that once produced platoons of qualified and proud mechanics and electricians have disappeared. Why train people, they ask, when we can find qualified people in the labor market? But as many are discovering, there are no longer enough qualified people out there to find and hire, or they come at a much higher cost.

The point is that we are not training nearly enough people needed to fill these roles and replace tomorrow's empty jobs. And if we don't reverse this trend—and fast—the growing middle-skills gap they leave behind will have unhappy consequences for all concerned. For businesses with too few capable workers, this will mean promising new projects left on the shelf and missed opportunities for growth. For individuals without the right kind of marketable skills, the consequences will be lower lifetime earnings and extended periods of unemployment. For our communities, the middle-skills gap will contribute to a host of ills: from reduced tax revenues to a whole myriad of social issues.

If we continue on the course of inaction, the middle-skills gap will also have consequences for our national economy and our competitiveness in the world. For example, there is much talk going on in businesses and in the political arena across the United States today of a coming renaissance in manufacturing and a "reshoring" of jobs once lost to Asia. It has, in fact, already begun in a small way, often led by companies you'll meet later in this book. This new era of U.S. manufacturing will look much different from the one that preceded it. There will be more reliance on specialized skills in robotics, process control, and planning. Mass production will give way to mass customization, which is more reliant on mastery of computer-controlled systems. People who want a place in this evolving workforce will be asked to upgrade their skill sets and perform at higher levels than ever before.

The takeaway is clear: Economic vitality on both the community level and beyond requires a large population of employed citizens working in great jobs that make a difference outside of the cubicle or corner office: auto technicians, bookkeepers, carpenters, caterers, chefs, computer techs, electricians, horticulturalist laboratory technicians, health workers, heavy equipment operators, machinists, mechanics, physical therapists, plumbers, and welders, to name just a few. We simply will not have enough of these people if we hold to our current mindset that assumes a successful career path hinges on the attainment of a college degree, and if we don't start embracing the alternative paths of vocational and skills-based education—and fast. Conversations about revitalizing industries such as manufacturing are exciting but moot if the conversations don't focus on the people who will build the nimble factories of the future. Who will operate them and repair those amaz-ing robots when they break down? Who will provide the training and education to prepare people and launch them into new and emerging-skills careers?

Put simply, closing the middle-skills gap will require the collaborative efforts of educational institutions, pri-vate employers, and government. Yet, until recently, in the United States in particular, collaborative models like these have been slow to catch on. Too many companies continue to follow a "buy not build" strategy to recruit-ment and employment, choosing to compete for talent in the open market rather than invest long-term in a plan of skilling up their own workers. This shortsighted strategy bites where it hurts, however, when demand for skilled hands outstrips supply, as it has today in many industry sectors—and as it is likely to remain in the future, when the world's developed economies will face a predicted shortfall of forty-five million middle-skilled workers.[8]

At the same time, vocational training has been rapidly disappearing from our high schools ever since its high-water mark in the 1950s. The situation has reached the point that the Organization of Economic Cooperation and Development has placed the United States at the bot-tom of its twenty-nine-country study of workplace pre-paredness among high school graduates. As you'll read about more in later chapters, vocational education has become both marginalized and stigmatized, as every-one from educators to parents and even employers seem unable to part with the idea that success depends upon going to college. For these people, "vocational" means "minimum-wage and menial work." This is the mindset I hope to debunk in this book.

The Way Forward

Luckily, there are many reasons to believe that profound change is on the horizon. For every worker who can't find work, there exists a company with vacant jobs to be filled. And for every job seeker without the right skills, there exist myriad accessible and inexpensive opportunities to acquire those skills.

More good news is that educators, companies, and communities are beginning to increase access to the middle-skills education and training that is the cornerstone of a more stable and secure economic future. Indeed, the schools and companies that you'll read about in these pages—including IBM, P-TECH, Whole Foods Market, Siemens, Aviation High, Central Piedmont Community College, Volkswagen, JPMorgan Chase & Co., STIHL Inc., Starbucks, and the Citi Foundation—are creating powerful new initiatives that I believe will go a long way toward closing the jobs-skills gap, reducing unemployment and ensuring more prosperous livelihoods for the next generation of workers. As Rana Foroohar reported in a 2014 *Time* magazine cover story, there is a structural change in the economy afoot—one that favors technology-based and STEM (science, technology, engineering, and math) skills and one that is not only making career-oriented education more and more attractive to young people, but also making tech-savvy young people more attractive to companies and employers. "And there are a growing number of blue chips, like IBM, that believe getting involved in education is good for both their long- and short-term business models: it simultaneously addresses their skilled-labor shortage and helps build a stronger middle class that will spend on their products in the future," Foroohar wrote. Enterprises like these are taking the right action and opening up a whole new world of opportunity to job seekers and the workforce.

From my work leading an organization dedicated to helping people find a rewarding career path, I know there is much that we can do to solve the jobs-skills problem. I know that our current unskilled or underskilled workers—be they young high school or college graduates searching for solid footing, midcareer people looking for greater job satisfaction, or displaced or downsized workers of all ages longing to pursue a lifelong career dream—aren't destined for a life of pumping gas, flipping burgers, or waiting for the welfare checks to come in the mail. I know that there do exist myriad accessible and affordable alternatives to the traditional four-year college pathway—from vocational high school programs to occupational associate degrees, apprenticeships, and more—that will equip these learners with the practical and marketable skills that pave the road to well-paid careers. And I know there are many feasible solutions that we as a society can take to close the skills gap for businesses and open the door to solid middle-class incomes for millions.

Holy Headshot!

Intellectually, I know this because the data shows it. Emotionally, I know it because of stories like Douglas's. If you are an aspiring actor or entertainer in New York City, you may have heard the name Douglas Gorenstein. Anyone who aims to break into the theater, film, or television in New York City needs a first-class set of "headshots." Basically like a curriculum vitae for performers, a headshot is both a résumé and calling card for auditions and publicity, and in New York City, Douglas Gorenstein is the go-to headshot photographer. Douglas was voted "Favorite Headshot Photographer in New York" by the readers of *Backstage,* the actors' news magazine. Douglas served as the on-set headshot and still photographer for the television show *Celebrity Apprentice,* handles performance photography for the Dramatists Guild and major New York theater companies, and landed a coveted gig as the photographer for the *Tonight Show* starring Jimmy Fallon. He's even written a book (coauthored with *Tonight Show* writer Patrick Borelli) called *Holy Headshot!*: a collection of the world's funniest, craziest headshots of real actors. Douglas has achieved all this success—and more—without ever having finished college or earning a traditional degree.

While Douglas may not have a college diploma, what he does have is an interesting and rewarding life. He works every day with remarkable people and is doing work that he loves. And he's well paid. Not bad for a man who strayed far from the standard path through life.

No one who knew him growing up would have predicted Douglas's success as a photographer. He didn't fiddle obsessively with cameras as a kid and he didn't study photography in college. Photography was something he pursued only after trying other lines of work. But once the camera bug bit him, Douglas experimented, took several courses, and built his skills through hands-on practice. Those skills, an artistic sensibility, and his ability to get along well with people helped Douglas to build his business, earn a substantial income, and pursue an interesting and enjoyable line of work.

Douglas's artistic sense was a product of his childhood in the suburban Detroit area. His father, an anesthesiologist, and his mother, an artist, frequently took Douglas and his younger brother to concerts and the theater and encouraged his creativity. He still recalls how, as a seven-year-old, he received from his father a box filled with a variety of hats belonging to different professions. "He gave me the box and said, 'Dougie, now you can become any character you want to be.'"

So it's not surprising that Douglas developed an interest in the arts and eventually entered Wayne State University in Detroit with the intention of majoring in theater. "I was passionate about acting and performing," he said. But with the wanderlust that drives many young men, he dropped out after two years and went off to explore Australia and New Zealand. Less than a year later he returned and settled in New York City, where he was accepted at the New Actors Workshop, a two-year nondegree program where he studied with Mike Nichols, George Morrison, Paul Sills, and Gene Hackman. Upon graduating, Douglas decided to pursue his acting dreams. He auditioned for and was made a member of the Actors Studio, where he was taken under the wing of Academy Award–winning actress Ellen Burstyn. To pay the bills during his many years of plying the acting trade, he collected and resold vintage clothing. (He had a special fondness for unique hats.)

"From a creative standpoint," he recalls, "acting was very satisfying," but it didn't go a long way toward providing a steady livelihood. "I was a good actor," he explains, "but I was terrible at the business of acting." So at age thirty-one, he decided to find a new vocation. But what? He definitely wasn't the kind of guy who'd be happy with a nine-to-five office job. Then Ellen Burstyn gave him some advice that made a huge impression. She reminded Douglas that he was a creative person, and that, as she put it, "Creative people need creative ways to make a living."

After a year of soul searching he woke up one morning with an epiphany: "I bet I'd be a great photographer."

During his time in the theater he had been around lot of them. He'd watched what they did and understood how good photography could help actors succeed. "I thought to myself, 'I could do that; I could learn that craft and I bet I'd enjoy it.'" So with a professional film camera borrowed from his mother, he began experimenting, taking pictures of his actor friends. He also enrolled in several courses at the International Center of Photography. He didn't follow the full two-year program, but that training, plus lots of practice, got Douglas off to a good start.

Over the years, Douglas learned from his mistakes and got progressively more skilled. After five years he felt that he had mastered his craft, and today he enjoys a career that is well-paying, fun, and full of exciting new challenges. When I asked him what he would tell others who were at inflection points in their careers, Douglas Gorenstein offered this advice: "Pursue your passion wherever it leads. If that means going through a vocational training program, do it. If it means going to college, go for it. Just follow your passion. Wear your chosen hat."

If we want to scale success stories like Douglas's through the ranks of today's job seekers, we have work to do! Now is the time to change attitudes about career success, challenge assumptions about college for everyone, and embrace the nontraditional and innovative educational opportunities that will equip our nation's workers with the skills companies actually need—and in the process prop up entire industries and put millions of Americans on the path to successful and satisfying careers.

||||||||||||||||||||||||||||||||||||||||||||||||||||||||||||||||||||||||||||||||||||||||||||||||||||||||||||||||||

WHERE ARE TOMORROW'S JOBS?

Not sure which occupational areas are in demand and how much they pay? One source of information is "Five Ways That Pay Along the Way to the B.A.," by Anthony Carnevale, Tamara Jayasundara, and Andrew R. Hanson, at the Georgetown Center for Education and the Workforce. That report's appendix identifies the top-paying middle-skills jobs in ten occupational groups, their wage levels, and projected future growth rates. It's available at no cost at http://cew.georgetown.edu/ctefiveways.

For U.S. readers, a more extensive and timely source of information on jobs is the *Occupational Outlook Handbook*, which is updated annually by the U.S. Bureau of Labor Statistics (www.bls.gov/ooh). Check it out. Get the facts.

||||||||||||||||||||||||||||||||||||||||||||||||||||||||||||||||||||||||||||||||||||||||||||||||||||||||||||||||||

2

Unskilling a Nation

We've read about how too many young people today finish school woefully lacking in both practical, marketable skills, as well as the soft skills needed to secure a job, collaborate on a team, make a presentation, and successfully navigate in the real workplace. But who exactly is to blame?

It would be easy enough to lay blame at the hands of the educational system for failing to prepare our youth for the world of work. Yet I believe it's less helpful to debate blame than to collectively accept responsibility for failing to prepare the nation's youth. At the same time we must remember that our schools haven't always neglected to equip our young people with practical and technical skills that companies need—that, in fact, America has a rich history of vocational education, dating all the way back to Colonial times. As the country developed, so did its demands for societal, economic, and educational change, bringing about multiple and continuous reforms, mandates, and initiatives on how best to prepare young adults for the future.

Some of these initiatives have recognized the value of vocational education in keeping America competitive and people employed. Others have hindered the nation's ability to provide its youth with a skills-based education and, in turn, reduced their chances of finding good jobs. Over the past fifty years, the demand for social, economic, and educational change has engendered a steep decline in vocational learning—that is, what we typically think of as "shop class"—at the high school level, unseating it from its role as a mainstay of the curriculum and relegating it to the fringes of the system. Has vocational education in America lost its way?

More than twenty years ago, a Massachusetts Institute of Technology study of national competitiveness, "Made in America," may have answered that question when it issued this warning: "Without major changes in the ways schools and firms train workers over the course of a lifetime, no amount of microeconomic fine-tuning or technological innovation will be able to produce significantly improved economic performance and a rising standard of living."

Making these changes will take some work. First it will require a shift in our definition of a classroom from rows of chairs or an auditorium-style setting to research facilities, factory floors, manufacturing plants, and other actual workplaces. It will require major investments in state-of-the-art equipment and education environments that will provide hands-on learning experiences that go far beyond the abilities of teaching assistants or adjunct faculty. It will require us to challenge the "college for everyone" mindset and the prevailing misconception that the only path to career success entails stories about how one spent his or her four (if not five or six) years in an academic setting. And, finally, it will require us to acknowledge and learn from our mistakes, and restore and re-embrace the rich tradition of vocational learning that once made this country great.

Falling Apart

Vocational education, which can most simply be defined as accredited training in job-related and technical skills, has a long and respected history in the United States, dating back to 1642, when the Massachusetts Bay Colony required youths apprenticing with masters of a trade to learn reading and writing. During and after the Civil War, proponents of vocational education broadened their mission, and by 1868, the first private trade school had opened in Virginia. By the early 1890s trade schools had cropped up in several major cities, including New York and Philadelphia, and in 1917, the federal government officially declared its commitment to making occupational training part of public school curricula with the passage of the Smith-Hughes Act, which helped shape, monitor, and govern vocational education programs in each state.

Vocational education—more commonly known as shop class—entered U.S. public school systems in a big way after World War I. The country's railroads, factories, and construction enterprises were booming, and more skilled hands were needed to keep up the momentum. The model of vocational training developed in Germany was of particular interest to educators and governments on both sides of the Atlantic; Germany's industrial and military prowess had expanded remarkably since the 1870s, and many observers at the time attributed that prowess to its workers, whose reputation for skill, precision, and exacting standards was high. As the director of the British Technology Institute remarked in 1914, "In no other way can the phenomenal advance of the German nation be explained."

In post–World War I America, government commissions, lawmakers, and industry groups pushed hard for vocational education in secondary schools, and they got it. Vocational education (more recently rebranded as career technical education, or CTE) was eventually offered in most American high schools, and their curricula were usually formulated in consultation with the local businesses that would employ school graduates. Some jurisdictions, Massachusetts being a notable example, rolled out more than two dozen CTE-dedicated high schools, several of which specialized in agriculture, a booming industry at the time.

Through the 1950s, the heyday of U.S. manufacturing, America's high schools turned out millions of young people each year who had received some measure of job-related training as part of their education. Most American high school students followed more or less the same educational path—one that supplemented the traditional reading, writing, and arithmetic with vocational and job-ready skills. But in the late 1950s, vocational education began to veer off on a second track. America's high schools still provided millions of young people with job-related training, but while these students were taking bookkeeping, auto mechanics, wood shop, metal shop, electronics, and other practical courses, their college-bound peers busied themselves with a traditional curriculum that included Latin, creative writing, and a heavy dose of science and math. In effect, two different high school populations operated under the same roof. The students sat alongside each other in the required introductory courses such as civics, history, English literature, and so on. They participated together on sport teams and in other school activities. Yet each was on a very different trajectory. This "tracking," as it was called, did not sit well with many educators and parents. There was, and continues to be, the sense that students were assigned to one track or another on the basis of social/economic status—the wealthier students automatically placed on the college track while their working-class peers were placed in courses designed to prepare them for more hands-on blue-collar careers—rather than aptitude and ability.

For a society that prided itself on its economic mobility, tracking smacked of class stratification, social immobility, and even racism. And for many, it still does today. Strangely, even at a time when everyone—including anti-trackers—supports the idea of lifelong learning, there's a mistaken assumption that young people who pursue vocational education will be trapped in an educational and socioeconomic black hole from which a higher reach is impossible. This is not the case. In fact, the majority of tradespeople and vocationally trained people are quite upwardly mobile; many continue their educations through additional training and certification, often going on to earn associate degrees and pursuing well-paying professional careers.

Yet the objections to tracking have only intensified as the pervasive "college for everyone" idea grows in popularity. As the Urban Institute's Robert Lerman once observed, "Vocational content in schools attracted opposition by many in the progressive education movement. . . . In the U.S. educational system, 'vocationalism' has long been suspected of an antidemocratic education policy."[1] Joe Klein, a columnist for *Time* magazine, put it more bluntly: "Vocational education used to be where you sent the dumb kids or the supposed misfits who weren't suited for classroom learning," and, as the civil rights movement gathered force, it served "as a form of segregation—a convenient dumping ground for minority kids."[2] By the end of the 1950s, what was once a perfectly respectable, even mainstream, educational path came to be viewed as a punitive or remedial track designed to hold minority and working-class students back. In short it had become, as the *Economist* magazine put it, "America's most sneered-at high-school program."[3]

Thus, in the 1950s, vocational education in the United States—and, to a lesser extent, in Europe—began its relative decline, though the industrial sector of the economy was expanding. The next period to experience a substantial contraction, with a 44 percent drop in students specializing in vocational education, was 1982 through 1994, as Western companies began outsourcing production to Asia. The number of vocational credits taken by high schoolers continued to slide between 1994 and 2009, as many young people were seduced by the dramatic rise in compensation for knowledge economy jobs in fields such as computer science and investment banking. And the decline has continued since. Today, only 2 percent of U.S. high school students concentrate in vocational educational programs, compared to almost 50 percent of their peers in Europe's most economically competitive nations.[4]

The decline can be somewhat attributed to the shrinking manufacturing sector, but the "college for everyone" doctrine embraced by parents, educators, and government has greatly accelerated its demise. Yet the notion that every high school student should pursue a track leading directly to college is flawed in many ways. First is the simple variance in skills and aptitudes that I mentioned earlier. We all know individuals who seem to have a natural intelligence, ability, or affinity—or a passion, in many cases—for mechanical things, for numbers, for artistic expression, for music, or for any one of the dozens of skills not taught in a traditional classroom. Who doesn't know a neighbor's teenager who makes broken items new, and makes it look easy? Or the classmate who has been onstage or working behind the scenes in every school play, or has excelled in three different sports? What about the person working in the paint, hardware, or decorating store with an uncanny sense of which colors, textures, and shapes go together? Harvard professor Howard Gardner has written about these unique abilities in his widely read work on multiple intelligences,[5] the primary ones being visual-spatial, bodily kinesthetic, musical, interpersonal, intrapersonal, linguistic, and mathematical-logical.

Yet despite the evidence that we as humans possess many different traits, for decades our Western educational system has favored those that involve logical and mathematical analysis and the ability to combine words into clear sentences and coherent paragraphs. Students who are good at these—and who have respectable study habits—get good grades and do well on standardized tests. As do those who can memorize names, dates, and facts and recite them under examination conditions. They are ready-made for the college pathway. Yet, whether college will prepare them for viable careers will depend on a range of life choices, including what they study (as anyone who majored in anthropology or philosophy will confirm).

Of course, these skills are valuable, but what about the students who are not left-brained logical-analytical types, whose talents or interests don't align with the "intelligences" valued by too many "college for everyone" promoters? Or those who simply are not very good at learning while sitting all day in a traditional classroom setting? Most of these students will still be urged by guidance counselors and admissions officers, or expected by well-intentioned parents, to follow the path to a four-year college degree. Some will find their place and meet the collegiate challenge, but most will either drift along or drop out. According to Kenneth Gray, a professor of education at Pennsylvania State University, "A comparison of their post-secondary plans with their academic records and labor market prospects suggests that most of these young people are seriously adrift." Of those who beat the odds and earn degrees, Professor Gray estimates that one-third or more will end up in jobs they could have had without a four-year college degree.[6]

California, a bellwether state in so many ways, is an exemplar of this national decline in vocational education. In 2013, faced with a budget deficit, the Los Angeles Unified School System, with more than six hundred thousand students, slated almost all its shop classes for elimination by year-end. And in January 2013, the similarly cash-strapped Long Beach City College—a two-year community/vocational college—cut eleven programs, almost all in vocational areas: auto body technology, aviation maintenance, audio production, interior design, welding, automotive technology, real estate, photography, air conditioning/refrigeration/heating, diesel mechanics, and carpentry. Programs like these are expensive to operate, and so they are often the first to go when budgets are tight. These decisions reflect a statewide, and increasingly nationwide, trend by which high school shop classes are being dropped to save money and to make room for courses designed to ensure that graduating seniors are prepared for the first year of course work in the state's four-year university system.

The problem with this *seemingly* reasonable allocation of assets is that only around 30 percent of those high school graduates will go on to that system. And, sadly, the outcome for the other 70 percent is grim; they will enter the workforce with no practical skills training.

The landmark study on the mindset of college for everyone as the preferred pathway was conducted at the Harvard Graduate School of Education. Its authors summed it up this way:

> Our current system places far too much emphasis on a single pathway to success: attending and graduating from a four-year college after completing an academic program of study in high school. Yet as we've seen, only 30 percent of young adults successfully complete this preferred pathway, despite decades of efforts to raise that number. And too many of them graduate from college without a clear conception of the career they want to pursue, let alone a pathway for getting there.[7]

It must also be noted that there is growing evidence that the academic track is not meeting young people's needs. Studies show that it is not only failing to adequately prepare our nation's young people for the workplace; it's also failing to prepare them for college. In 2011 only 24 percent of high school graduates met the ACT's college readiness benchmarks in English, reading, math, and science,[8] yet more than half of those grads entered two- or four-year colleges the following September, putting them at a huge disadvantage—and one that will only grow—from day one. Moreover, because high schools are increasingly failing to prepare students with the academic skills that will be required of them once they enter a postsecondary institution, those institutions have had to direct scarce financial resources into programs of "remedial education" that try to bring students up to college-level abilities. Roughly one-third of incoming college freshmen now require one or more remedial courses that do not count toward graduation. Worse yet, the remedial courses have only increased the likelihood of a student's graduating by 8 to 15 percent. What would be accomplished if the enormous expenditures of time, money, and teaching resources spent for remedial instruction were instead directed into skill-building education? Researchers Kenneth Gray and Edwin Herr put it this way: "If these large numbers of students are not prepared to do baccalaureate degree academic work, then maybe— just maybe—they should be doing something else. And if given some legitimate, socially valued alternatives that make economic sense, perhaps many of these students *would* do something else."[9]

Despite all this evidence, the "college for everyone" doctrine persists, partly thanks to studies concluding that college graduates receive substantially higher lifetime earnings (nearly $1 million higher) than do peers who fail to complete high school. Yet these income studies have several problems. First, they are backward looking, telling us more about *past* income differentials rather than what we are seeing now and may see in the future. The past is one thing. The present is another. And the future is anyone's guess. It has become clear that a college degree is not packing the earnings or employability punch it once had, especially for nontechnical baccalaureates. One reason is oversupply. Every year the United States produces around 1.8 million four-year college graduates. But for every one hundred of these graduates, there exist only an estimated fifty-seven jobs that *require* a four-year college degree.[10] This means that 43 percent of grads will likely find themselves underemployed and underpaid, doing work that does not require their four years of postsecondary study, often for as little as minimum wage. The U.S. Bureau of Labor Statistics found, in fact, that 47 percent of currently employed college grads are in jobs that do not require a four-year degree. Worse, 37 percent are doing work for which only a high school degree is required.[11] Were all those years of study and tuition payment the best investment?

||||||||||||||||||||||||||||||||||||||||||||||||||||||||||||||||||||||||||||||||

HOW MANY COLLEGE GRADS?

Typically, more than 3.6 million students graduate from postsecondary U.S. institutions each year. For the 2013–14 school year, here's the breakdown:

943,000 associate degrees

1.8 million bachelor's degrees

778,000 master's degrees

177,000 doctoral degrees

Source: National Center for Educational Statistics, 2014.

||||||||||||||||||||||||||||||||||||||||||||||||||||||||||||||||||||||||||||||||

It's also important to note that comparisons in the earning power of high school versus college graduates are tricky and can be misleading because of tremendous variability in employability and earnings between majors. Not all college majors are created equal. When you get down to it, *what* a person studied in college is far more relevant to earning power than the fact that he or she earned a degree. For example, a 2013 study using data from 2010–11 found that unemployment for people who majored in architecture and information systems was 12.8 percent and 14.7 percent, respectively, while nursing grads faced a mere 4.8 percent unemployment. That's a huge spread. And the rate for non-college grads during those years? Just under 10 percent. Income differences across college majors are even more dramatic and go beyond the scope of this discussion, but from my review of all the numbers one thing is clear: In many fields and majors, a college degree doesn't always deliver the earning power it once did.

Moreover, while the incomes of bachelor's degree graduates skyrocketed between 1995 and the end of the decade, in 2000 they hit a brick wall, and have been in retreat ever since. For example, 2009 employment data in the state of Florida indicated that the recipient of bachelor's degrees from the state's public and private four-year schools earned *less,* on average, than did the state's community college graduates! And Florida is not an anomaly. In the state of Virginia, graduates with technical or occupational associate degrees currently outearn the state's bachelor's degree recipients by almost $2,500 per year.[12] And they don't carry nearly the student debt of their baccalaureate counterparts.

One reason for the dip in lifetime earnings among college graduates is the simple fact that many college graduates entering the job market aren't able to find any work at all. While people with degrees—as a population—continue to have an employment edge, that piece of paper is far from the guarantee of a job that it once was. In fact, nearly 54 percent of bachelor's degree holders under age twenty-five were unemployed or underemployed in 2011.

As just one example, let's look at one of the worst-hit groups in recent years: law school graduates. A law degree has historically been a ticket to high earnings—even great wealth. The same can no longer be said without qualification. In *The Lawyer Bubble,* Steven Harper, a law school professor, reveals that some forty-five thousand U.S. law students are awarded degrees each year, taking on an average of $100,000 in student loans in the process. Yet only *half* of them will find full-time jobs that require a law degree, and, of these, many are part-time positions as low-paid contract attorneys—a far cry from the glamorous six-figure job at a high-powered, well-respected law firm that a law degree once implied.

THE NEXT FINANCIAL CRISIS?

U.S. student loan debt at the beginning of 2014 exceeded $1 trillion and was rising. That put it well above total U.S. credit card debt, making it the largest category of unsecured credit. Could this enormous pile of IOUs result in a future financial meltdown—a reprise of the subprime mortgages meltdown of 2008–10? No one really knows. Student loans are disturbingly similar to the subprime mortgages in one important respect: They are made with no assessment of the borrower's ability to repay. This violates the most essential principle of good financial practices and, as we saw with the mortgage crisis, is a recipe for disaster. Currently, one in ten borrowers defaults on his or her federal student loan within the first two years. That figure is bound to worsen as millions of people fail to earn degrees or fail to achieve the postcollege incomes they were promised by the "college for everyone" doctrine.

Whether we'll see a meltdown or not, student loan debt is already throwing a monkey wrench into the economy. Young adults burdened by monthly debt payments are delaying home ownership and other big-ticket purchases, and cutting back on restaurant meals, vacation travel, and other forms of consumption that fuel a third of the national economy.

Another problem with college-versus-high-school earnings studies is that they do not account for the earnings differences between high school grads who receive vocational training as part of their secondary education, and the vast majority who receive none at all. Empirical and anecdotal evidence strongly indicates that young people who concentrate in career training education enjoy both higher employment rates and higher wages than do graduates from traditional academic high schools. Gray and Herr surmise that this is largely because CTE graduates are more likely to be working in positions that require prior skills. So while their counterparts are working in fast food or other low-wage jobs, CTE grads find their ways into the skilled trades, where labor demand and compensation are notably higher.

Finally, lifetime earnings studies fail to recognize higher education's well-kept secret: that almost *40 percent* of those who begin four-year degree programs in the United States fail to complete their studies and earn degrees. These young people have paid tuition and forfeited one or more income-earning years, and in the end they find themselves back at square one—often with a mountain of student loan debt to pay off and no degree to show for it. This is analogous to taking on a long-term mortgage but not getting to enjoy the benefits of owning a home.

If we want to significantly improve economic performance and produce a rising standard of living (as the MIT study put it), we need to bring practical learning—skillbuilding experiences such as those found in shop class and the best of vocational education tracks—back into the mainstream as they were prior to the 1950s and as they still are in Germany, Switzerland, Austria, and other nations where trade skills are honored and rewarded in the classroom and in the workplace.

Changing the "College for Everyone" Mindset

Luckily, not everyone in the educational establishment buys into the idea that tracking is an outdated, classist tool meant to keep those young people not interested in a four-year degree from reaching their full potential. Dr. Ronnie L. Booth, president of Tri-County Technical College in South Carolina, with decades of experience in educating young people, is one of the strongest voices in the chorus challenging the "college for everyone" concept. In his view, the educational practice of tracking provides the guidance and direction that some young people need as they negotiate the difficult transition between adolescence and adulthood, and between school and work life. As he told me, "You can track some people into a good career or track them to jail or to a life of poverty."

What he means is that many of the young people about whom the anti-trackers are most concerned are, ironically, at the greatest risk of going "off the tracks" with their lives. Here I'm talking about youngsters who are clearly adrift—young people who grow up in dysfunctional families, or in homes with no positive role models, or those living in two-income families with parents who are too busy working hard to pay the bills or too distracted by the daily routine to provide effective guidance. There are too many of these young people today searching for direction and the educational means to reach their career dreams, and they could all benefit from the skills conferred through the vocational track, and all the structure and support that go with it. Indeed, a study conducted at Ohio State University confirmed that at-risk youngsters are the greatest beneficiaries of vocational education because it does a better job of keeping them in school and engaged than the traditional high school curriculum. In the United States, so-called high-risk students are eight to ten times less likely to drop out of grades eleven and twelve if they are enrolled in a program of vocational education instead of a conventional high school one, and of those who concentrate in vocational training, 90 percent graduate versus the U.S. high school graduation rate of 75 percent.[13] The message behind these numbers is loud and clear. As a practical matter, staying in school and developing a marketable skill does more for these young people than just about anything that the college track has to offer.

For one thing, many of the practical skills learned in a high school shop class are later transferred to and appreciated in work-life situations—they have long-term hidden career value often not recognized by ninth or tenth graders. This was certainly the case for me. I'll never forget the woodworking class I took from Mr. Bernie Mitchell at age sixteen. Bernie (though I wouldn't have dared call him by his first name back then) was a military veteran and ran his shop with no-nonsense army-like precision. What he taught me about having the right attitude, being accurate in everything you do, and, most important, being accountable for your work has proved invaluable to me time and again over the course of my own career. The professional confidence and leadership skills I gained in that class served me well later on when I worked as a chef.

The golden rule of woodworking that Bernie drummed into our teenage brains—measure twice, cut once—turned out to be equally applicable to measuring ingredients as it had been to measuring two-by-fours, saving many a recipe from sure disaster.

All of which has left me wondering *why* high school students receive so little professional advice about careers in the trades or other occupations. Yes, the idea of studying screenwriting, anthropology, art history, or world history is appealing to many young people, but who is warning them about the limited employment opportunities in these fields, let alone all the work required to search out openings, get interviewed, land a job, and successfully perform every day? And who is helping the high school kids with poor or mediocre academic records understand the rigors of college classes and the different learning obstacles they will need to overcome in order to graduate? High school career centers don't seem to be doing a particularly good job; at the time of this writing almost 60 percent of high school counselors were still recommending college to students who tested in the *bottom* half of their classes.[14]

This is a travesty given that, as we'll read more about in later chapters, technical and vocational professions have the potential to offer higher pay, greater job security, and deeper job satisfaction than that attained by following the traditional academic track. It is time to give vocational education the recognition it deserves as a door to a viable and respectable career.

BLUE-COLLAR, WHITE-COLLAR,
NO-COLLAR WORKERS

For decades, blue-collar workers have been described as being in the trades, performing front-line, service-based jobs, while white-collar careers were characterized by sitting at a desk, be it in a cubicle or the corner office. The technology revolution changed colored collars to turtlenecks (think Steve Jobs), and for today's millennium workers, the dress code for many is "no collars." In the workplace of today (and of the future) a good job is no longer defined by what one wears—but rather by a worker's job satisfaction, experiences, and performance every day . . . although a professional appearance will always be a criteria for success.

Choosing the vocational education track early in life does not close the door to other academic or professional options, despite what many would have you believe. Tracking isn't a straitjacket. In fact, it can often be a springboard to greater educational and career advancement. I'm living proof of that, and I'm willing to bet that more than half the adult readers of this book are currently working in fields that have little or nothing to do with the academic course of study they chose when they were nineteen or twenty. Somehow we have all managed to successfully switch "tracks" in the course of our lives, be it by chance, choice, or corporate layoff. In Switzerland, where vocational education has far less stigma, 40 percent of all university graduates began on vocational tracks. And, as just one anecdotal example, when I spoke with Siemens USA president and CEO Eric Spiegel on the subject of track switching, he was quick to point out that one of his chief financial people had successfully changed tracks over the course of his career.

Don't get me wrong. If pursuing a four-year degree is something a new high school grad has their heart set on, or if they feel a real calling to pursue a career that *does* require a college education, I am their biggest champion. But the point I wish to make is that a traditional four-year stint in college is not the only option. It is about the right education, at the right time—for you! The doors to many other opportunities will begin to open once we broaden the definition of "postsecondary education" from just the word "college" to include the many alternate paths to learning: associate degree programs at community and technical colleges, certification programs, and apprenticeships, each of which will be discussed in more detail in subsequent chapters. But as long as parents, career advisers, and education policy makers believe that the word "academic" before the word "track" is the only sure pathway to a successful work life, millions of young adults will continue to be asked to step onto unrewarding career paths.

"BUT NOT FOR MY KID"

The public perceptions of careers in manufacturing are steeped in irony. Since 2009, the National Association of Manufacturers has conducted annual surveys to gauge public perceptions of the industry. In the latest of these (2012), the vast majority of respondents (90 percent) ranked manufacturing at the top of the list of important industries—above energy, health care, technology, and finance—and reported that they saw it as critical to their country's prosperity and security. Moreover, 80 percent thought that building a strong manufacturing base should be a national priority. But here's the twist. When asked if they would encourage their *own* children to enter this critical field, they answered: Decidedly not! Despite their stated belief in the virtue of a career in manufacturing, only 35 percent would embrace it as a viable option for their own children.

Knowledge Builds Power

Any parent or young person who wants to judge the power of vocational education to smooth the transition from school to work only has to look to the economically robust countries of Europe, where the benefits of learning a skills-based trade are still appreciated and supported by public policy, parents, and educators. According to a lengthy report from Harvard University's Graduate School of Education, "Most advanced nations place far more emphasis on vocational education than we do." In Austria, Denmark, Finland, Germany, the Netherlands, Norway, and Switzerland, the study reports, between 40 and 70 percent of young people opt for an educational program that typically combines classroom and on-the-job learning after completing grade nine or ten. It's no coincidence that unemployment rates for young people in these countries and other nations where vocational training is standard are roughly half of what we're suffering in the United States, the United Kingdom, Australia, and other countries where vocational education has been marginalized.

For an idea of what a robust vocational system *could* look like, we can look in particular to Germany, where vocational training is ingrained in the educational culture. Compared to the United States, where *one-half of 1 percent* of high school graduates become apprentices, three of every four German secondary school students complete paid internships or apprenticeships that combine on-the-job training with classroom instruction. This dual system of education includes both technical and more academic vocations, such as medical technology and banking. German apprentices spend three or four days each week training in a workplace and twelve hours each week in a vocational school, where one-third of their time is spent in the classroom and focused on general education, while the rest is spent on occupational education. For many students, the time spent in a work setting—be it a manufacturing plant, a bank, a restaurant kitchen, or a medical facility—is not only a welcome respite from passive classroom learning, it also provides them with everyday opportunities to work alongside and learn from skilled adults, in a setting where they can get a good sense of what they need to succeed in the real world of work. When they finish high school, the students graduate with the equivalent of a U.S. community college associate degree—and a lot of real-world experience. The effects on the overall economy are clear: At the time of this writing, youth unemployment was 7.7 percent in Germany versus 19.7 percent in the United Kingdom and 14.4 percent in the United States.

European vocational programs are more rigorous and relevant to actual workplace requirements than their U.S. equivalents. As a result of these high standards, graduates exit these programs not only faring better in the workforce but also better prepared to move on to more advanced studies in institutions of higher education and applied science (which they do, in significant numbers). And, of course, this isn't just good for the students; most observers of economic activity today credit Germany's vibrant manufacturing sector (as well as its low youth unemployment rate) to the robust skills of its workforce. When Britain's former prime minister Tony Blair asked German chancellor Angela Merkel why her country's economy was so strong, her answer was short and simple: "We still make things."

In the summer of 2013 I had the opportunity to travel to northern Germany to meet Felix Rauner, a professor of professional education at the University of Bremen. It is fitting that Rauner, like many academics I have met in Germany and Switzerland, began his working life in the technical trades—in his case, as an electrician. And as with many Europeans, his early trade education was no barrier whatsoever to an academic or professional career—a fact that detractors of vocational tracking should note. Rauner has become a leading authority on vocational education and training, having authored or coauthored more than 350 articles and thirty books on the subject. Rauner believes that the association among manufacturing, employment, and economic prosperity is clear and unambiguous. Vocational education and training at the high school level, in his view, is the foundation for all three.

Here in the United States, we would do well to learn from the Germans the value and advantages vocational education offers. They understand that the key to equipping their future workforce with the kinds of skills required to keep their economy (and, in particular, the manufacturing sector) vibrant is to start training that workforce early.

The best way to do this here is to revive the kinds of successful vocational programs that were a standard component of every American high school education prior to the 1950s. We need to bring skills-based learning back into the mainstream. Vocational education in the United States need not be perceived as a track for underachievers; it is a solid educational path for any young person seeking to acquire the competencies, confidence, and knowledge to launch a career—while at the same time contributing to a productive workforce and flourishing economy. In the chapters that follow you'll read more about the many doors that vocational education can open, and about the exciting opportunities available through pathways *other* than pursing the traditional four-year college degree.

Career and Technical High Schools and Skills Certifications

Back in early 2014, while doing research for this book, my family and I were spending the night at a hotel in Wayne, Pennsylvania, northwest of Philadelphia. In what has to be every parent's worst nightmare, we were awakened at four a.m. by the sound of my three-year-old young son, James, gasping for breath. By the time we got to him his lips were blue and he was frantically pulling at his throat. I checked for obstructions. Nothing. I immediately called 911 while my wife carried him down the fire stairs to the hotel lobby. An ambulance with an emergency medical technician and a paramedic aboard roared up in what seemed like less than two minutes and immediately took control of the situation.

"Looks like a severe croup attack," one of the medics told us, a condition that, as we learned later, can cause a life-threatening constriction of the airways in a young child. They quickly stabilized James and, with sirens blaring, whisked him off to the local hospital, where over the next few days he made a full recovery.

We never had a chance to thank those two heroes,

which got me thinking about other men and women who devote their working lives to saving others. Where do they acquire their know-how? What are their jobs like? I had the opportunity to learn the answers to those questions not long after through interviews with Dave Hohnstein and Chris Rodes, members of an air medical "strike team" employed by Air Evac Lifeteam.

Dave is a registered nurse, but his day-to-day job is unlike that of any nurse you've ever met. While many RNs work in a clinic or hospital setting, Dave does his work in the confines of a medical helicopter racing along at 130-plus miles per hour high above the treetops. Most of his patients are victims of car wrecks, farm accidents, strokes, heart attacks, burns, and other traumas that need a level one or two trauma team fast. For them, every minute counts. It's Dave and his paramedic teammate Chris's job to stabilize patient conditions during those critical minutes. Paramedics, I learned, do everything that EMTs do, but are also trained to give medications orally and intravenously, interpret electrocardiograms, and use other monitors and complex equipment. Because so many missions involve people with cardiac issues and serious injuries, Chris uses that advanced training regularly. But what makes Dave unique compared to other nurses is the fact that he didn't learn his lifesaving skills at a traditional nursing school, but rather through on-the-job experience and many hours of certificate training.

The daily routines of air medical personnel have much in common with those of firemen: lots of time waiting punctuated by periods of intense activity. During an "on" day they may get one or two calls. In the meantime, everyone keeps busy by maintaining the equipment, going through checklists, and working on the continuing education courses they need to maintain their many state licenses and certifications. Continuous learning is part of the job description. Dave enjoys and finds great satisfaction in his job. "When you work in a hospital, you don't always see the outcome of your work or know that you've made a difference," he said. "That's not the case here. I know that I've saved many lives." He also likes the pay, which is more than an RN in a local hospital or clinic earns.

Air Evac Lifeteam is the largest independently owned and operated membership-supported air ambulance service in the United States. It provides air medical transport from more than 115 bases across fifteen states, serving mostly medically underserved areas far from level one and two trauma centers. And its service area continues to grow.

Air Evac Lifeteam's fleet consists of more than 120 medically equipped Bell 206 Long Ranger and Bell 407 helicopters, the largest such fleet in the civilian world. Each aircraft carries a pilot, flight nurse, and flight paramedic. All are highly trained for their roles and are required to keep current in all relevant licenses and certifications through continued education.

Dave Hohnstein didn't follow the traditional path into his current job. Upon finishing high school he enlisted in the army, where he was trained in antiaircraft artillery. After eight years of active duty he left to join the air force reserves, which trained him as a medic. Eager to learn more, Dave completed an associate degree nursing program and went to work in hospital emergency rooms, initially in Mobile, Alabama, and later in Birmingham. That was where he came into contact with Air Evac Lifeteam. "I really liked the people and the company," he told me, "and I liked flying, so I signed on."

Though Dave was licensed as an RN in Alabama, before he could fly with Air Evac as a member of the strike team, he needed a license from every state in which he would operate (fourteen in his case) and certifications in several medical care specialties: basic life support for health care providers, advanced cardiac life support, pediatric advanced life support, and one of two different trauma life support certificates.

Dave's teammate, paramedic Chris Rodes, got into the air medical field through standard EMT training, which he completed at a community college near his home in eastern Tennessee. After four years of EMT work he went on to complete a paramedic program. In addition to classroom learning, his program required two hundred hours of "ride along" time, an internship, and passing a national certification test. Like Dave, he's required to keep his qualifications up-to-date. He stays motivated by the good pay, an interest in flying, and the simple knowledge that, as he put it to me, "you're making a difference" almost every day.

Dave and Chris and other emergency personnel—including the two who helped my son that night in Pennsylvania—may never earn the princely sums paid to doctors or surgeons, but they earn respectable and livable salaries—and they aren't saddled with hundreds of thousands of dollars in debt from medical school tuition. And, just like doctors, they get the satisfaction of saving lives every day—something that very few of us will ever experience.

In the previous chapter we read a bit about how vocational education at the high school level can start a student down a path to attaining valuable professional or occupational certifications, or attending a community or technical college for advanced training. Often referred to as high school-*plus,* this track can be a great choice for anyone with little desire to pursue a traditional baccalaureate education—for anyone who hasn't bought into the "college for everyone" myth. And high school studies focusing primarily on trade or technical skills can provide the basic tools to better equip a student who is *not* interested in postsecondary education—or not *yet* ready or interested—land that all-important first job.

TOMORROW'S JOBS FOR HIGH SCHOOL GRADS

What educational requirements will today's students need in tomorrow's job market? The Georgetown Center on Education and the Workforce has forecast that 28 percent of jobs in 2018 will require a high school degree. That's a large slice of the total job pie, but it's a lot smaller than it was in decades past. As our workforce becomes increasingly globalized and automated, it's a fair bet that skilled high school grads will fare better than their unskilled peers. The following chart shows the predicted jobs outlook by educational level in 2018.

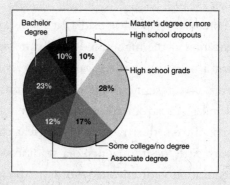

Source: Data from Anthony P. Carnevale, Nicole Smith, and Jeff Strohl, "Help Wanted: Projections of Jobs and Educational Requirements," Georgetown Center on Education and the Workplace.

Popular misconceptions hold that the earning potential for high school graduates without a four-year degree is generally disappointing—that the lack of a bachelor's degree is akin to a life sentence of low-wage, low-skill service jobs with limited advancement opportunities. Yet the reality is that vocational high school graduates with certifications and some work experience are not only highly employable, they often earn *higher* salaries than their counterparts who graduate from traditional high schools and complete a few years of college—often even higher than college graduates without any skills training. One study that looked at incomes ten to fifteen years after graduation found that people who had at least two years of vocational high school education earned as much as the average college graduate, and at a fraction of the cost! Another study—this one by the U.S. Department of Labor—came to the same conclusion: "Workers with less education, but who are employed in jobs that require special skills or training, earn as much as [four-year] college graduates who do not require [skills] training to get their jobs."[1]

To see the power of vocational high school education—or "high school–plus" in action, I paid a visit to a school where real, practical, job-ready skills are being taught, and where graduating students are being positioned for success in the workforce.

Minuteman Regional High School

The state of Massachusetts is home to many world-class educational institutions—and I'm not just talking about MIT and Harvard. One of them, Minuteman Regional High School, is located in Lexington, Massachusetts, just a short walk from where "the shot heard round the world" triggered the American Revolution. As you may recall from your own high school education, on April 17, 1775, British soldiers marched through the night from Boston. Their destination: the rural hamlet of Concord, where they expected to find and confiscate cannons and powder stockpiled by hostile New England colonists. At daybreak they arrived in the town of Lexington, where a small band of "Minutemen," the local militia, barred their way. In the skirmish that followed, the red coats scattered their amateur opponents and continued on to Concord, along what is now called "Battle Road" and the current site of Minuteman Regional.

Battle Road today is a clay lane within Minute Man National Historic Park. The road and the remaining homesteads of the period have been restored to their original appearance, and livestock graze in adjacent meadows bordered by rustic stone walls and split rail fences. Thousands of visitors to the park drive past the entrance to Minuteman Regional every month, oblivious to the sixty-five-acre campus tucked away in a beautiful setting of woodlands and marshes that was covered with freshly fallen snow on the morning of my visit. This public school provides CTE (career technical education) to more than seven hundred high school students from Lexington and dozens of surrounding communities who opt for an alternative to the traditional high school in their own communities. Minuteman is not an anomaly, but rather part of a statewide system of twenty-six CTE-focused high schools and three agricultural campuses that many educators consider a model of best practice in career technical education.

Michelle Roche, Minuteman's CTE director, generously arranged for me to meet with her, Superintendent-Director Dr. Ed Bouquillon, and other coordinators to learn more about the school's curriculum and the secret to its success in preparing young people for productive futures. Minuteman's approach is successful by any reasonable yardstick of performance: 100 percent of seniors pass the state's rigorous proficiency test; 95 percent of students graduate; 65 percent go on to postsecondary education, and those that do, according to Superintendent-Director Dr. Ed Bouquillon, are twice as likely to finish their collegiate programs as their counterparts from traditional high schools in Massachusetts. One year following graduation, *95 percent* of Minuteman grads are either working, in college, or in the armed forces. Even more remarkable, 48 percent of Minuteman's young people are classified as "special needs" students: individuals with physical or other learning disabilities.

Minuteman's curriculum integrates traditional academic studies (English language arts, math, and science and technology) with vocational courses in three general categories: trades and transportation; bioscience and engineering; and human, business, and commercial services. These broad categories contain many occupation-oriented disciplines: auto mechanics, welding, marketing, hospitality, culinary arts, medical technology, environmental engineering, and more—twenty in all. Each has an advisory board that includes eight to ten relevant local employers. That connection with the employer community assures that students are taught real-world skills with direct, practical applications. During the first half of the freshman year, students can sample each of the twenty occupational areas for two days to get a feel for what interests them and fits best with their aspirations. Having an opportunity to sample different disciplines has real value. "It's not unusual," said school CTE director Michelle Roche, "for young people to come here thinking that they'd like to be one thing only to discover that their real calling is in a different field." The first year sampling period gives them an opportunity to make a more informed career decision.

Once they reach their sophomore year, students select a major and generally focus on it for the remaining three years even as they take traditional academic courses in math, English, science, and so forth. This marriage of academic and vocational courses has an interesting twist. Students alternate each week between them; in other words, for week one they'll be immersed in American literature and other traditional courses for six hours each day; week two will find them in the woods with their environmental engineering instructor, or in a computer lab learning how to design with computer-aided software, and so on. "Kids love that structure," said Michelle. "Instead of sitting in a desk all day they're on their feet, moving around, doing things. That's one of the reasons they come here."

Ron Marino, coordinator of the school's co-op program, cited another attraction. "Some kids are not academic learners. They learn by doing." These individuals, he observes, might not be very good at learning mathematics in the traditional classroom setting, "but they pick it up as they learn carpentry or plumbing, where they have to understand angles, how to measure in fractions and decimal, and so forth." Minuteman graduates leave the school with a high school diploma, one or more certifications, a foundation in the academic core of math, science, English, and history, and a "major" in one of the twenty CTE disciplines offered by the school: bioengineering, drafting, horticulture and landscaping, cosmetology, telecommunications, and robotics/automation, among others. In short, they leave high school ready for postsecondary education or for work.

You cannot help but notice the emphasis on skill building and learning by doing as you walk about the Minuteman campus. In addition to its many labs and workshops, there's a student-run salon where staff and visitors can get their hair done, an auto repair shop where students will tune up your car's ignition system, a bakery where students will sell you fresh pastries, and a mini shopping mall run by future businessmen and -women getting a hands-on education in management or business. There's also a café—aptly named the Fife and Drum— where aspiring chefs will fix you a nice meal.

Juniors and seniors with acceptable academic records have even more opportunities to learn in real-world situations, thanks to the school's extensive cooperative program and internships at local health care centers. Some 22 percent of Minuteman's seniors participate in the co-op program, in which they work for upward of thirty hours per week (during "shop" weeks), earning CTE course credits and, in most cases, $10 to $12 per hour. This is far from a cap on their earning power; in fact, the positive impact of this type of directed work experience on future income has been well documented by studies showing that such experience raises a young person's employability and improves access to more formal training—which leads to better positions and higher pay.[2]

One of the more interesting features of the school's curriculum is its small business entrepreneurship course, which every Minuteman regional student is required to complete. Entrepreneurship training in the United States is all the rage in undergraduate and MBA programs these days, but is still uncommon at the high school level. It makes perfect sense, however, for CTE students to learn the fundamentals of entrepreneurship. After all, many will eventually work in restaurants, auto repair shops, diagnostic laboratories, electrical contracting firms, or the building and construction trades—all fertile grounds for upstart, small, locally owned businesses. So it's a safe bet that many of today's students will want to become small or even large business owners once they've gotten some experience under their belts. Minuteman's entrepreneurship course prepares them well by teaching them practical skills, such as how to identify and target a customer market, assess the competitive landscape, obtain financing, and develop a pro forma profit and loss statement. By the end of the course, every student has developed a personal résumé and a comprehensive business plan that reflects his or her occupational specialty.

Unlike in a traditional high school, Minuteman students can also earn industry-recognized certificates in dozens of occupational areas, including marketing, health care, horticulture, and robotics. All students graduate with at least one certificate—a base-level safety certificate issued by the federal Office of Safety and Health Administration—and many obtain a second certificate, if not more, making them more work-ready and attractive to employers, which often leads to higher starting wages. For students entering certain fields, the hours of instruction and work experience they log while at Minuteman fulfill some of the professional licensing requirements that will boost their incomes even higher. It is telling that, unlike at traditional high schools, where success is measured by how many graduates go on to college, CTE schools evaluate their success by how well their young people make the school-to-work transition.

Contrary to the belief that the vocational education track limits a person's future options or levels of achievement, the integration of academic course work, occupational training, and the opportunity to earn professional certifications gives Minuteman graduates a solid platform from which they can move directly into a career, an apprenticeship (often starting one or two levels above beginning apprentices), or even to a two- or four-year college; many pathways are open to them. In this sense, degrees awarded by Minuteman and similar CTE institutions are "stackable," that is, graduates can add other degrees and certifications from community colleges and/or from apprenticeships or certificate training programs on top of whatever CTE credits or certification they earned at the high school level. That forward flexibility flies in the face of the tracking concerns of so many parents, educators, and school counselors discussed in the last chapter.

Students are not the only group of people in the community served by Minuteman. The school's menu of occupational certificate programs is deliberately tailored to the employment needs of local industry, and new high-value courses that address emerging training needs are periodically added. One example of the latter is Minuteman's course in biomanufacturing, the brainchild of Ed Bouquillon and Bill Ciambrone of Shire Human Genetic Therapies. By pooling their respective talent and resources, Minuteman and Shire developed a program that has managed to train seventy-five adults in the unique skill needs of a local business. "We do things like this," said Bouquillon, "because we're not just a school, we're part of the economic development of this area. That's what's distinctive about voc-ed."

In other words, while most school districts around the

United States have allowed career technical education to decline, Minuteman and its peers in the twenty-six-school Massachusetts system of CTE-focused high schools have strengthened it and made it relevant to the demands of a changing economy. As a result, most of their graduates, as one research team put it, "leave high school better equipped than most college-preparatory students."[3] That's high praise given that a nationwide survey of employers found that 39 percent of high school graduates lacked even entry-level skills and that 45 percent were ill prepared to advance beyond entry-level positions.[4] Schools like Minuteman are a primary reason why some have described the Massachusetts system as the "Cadillac" of U.S. vocational education.

Happily, this is not just a Massachusetts phenomenon; vocational certificate programs like these are cropping up across the nation. South Carolina is another state known for its innovative approach to skills-oriented education. At the Career and Technology Center high school in Pickens County, South Carolina, for example, students can earn college-level course credits in English, statistics, and a few other areas thanks to a collaboration between the high school and nearby Tri-County Technical College. Those credits put graduates on a faster track to associate or baccalaureate degrees. And like Minuteman, this South Carolina high school assures that every graduate leaves with a certificate recognized nationally by the U.S. Office of Safety and Health Administration—one that saves a future employer $500 in training costs, according to CTC high school director Ken Hitchcock, thus making those graduates more attractive to companies than their certificate-less peers.

Indeed, employer demand for students with high school–level vocational training is high in areas across the country—to the point where local employers actively recruit them prior to graduation. Portland, Oregon's Vigor Industrial, a shipbuilder, is one of them. Like thousands of industrial enterprises, Vigor is struggling to add new talent to its aging skilled workforce. So it recruits high school students from shop classes to train and work as painters, welders, and machinists. The first stage at Vigor is a paid summer intern program. Interns who demonstrate proficiency and the right attitude toward work are offered permanent jobs in the shipyard paying good wages.

Not every town or city has a CTE-focused high school like Minuteman, or a school-to-work program like Vigor's, but they are not unique. To find something similar in your community, ask your high school or community college counselors. Or go a step further: Call the human resources department at a local business you are interested in and ask, "Where do you look for skilled talent?" These opportunities won't be hard to find with just a little bit of legwork.

Occupational Vocational Certificate Programs

If your high school years are behind you, don't worry; vocational and skills-oriented high school programs like these aren't the only place to attain technical or occupational certifications. Far from it; in fact, postsecondary certificate programs are an increasingly popular practical pathway to skills-based careers and higher incomes.

Certificate programs offer concentrated training in hundreds of specialized fields and are perhaps the fastest and most effective way of building marketable skills. Most can be completed in less than a year, and those who complete them are awarded a certificate—sometimes called a "professional designation" or "trade certification"—that opens the door to potential employment or career advancement and change. The cost of certificate programs ranges widely, depending on their duration and the institutions offering them, but they are all substantially cheaper than a four- or even a two-year degree. The digital arts and design certificate program at the University of California, Riverside, for example, consists of 150 hours of instruction, and fees total around $3,990 and include books and some design software. At a community college in Massachusetts, you can be certified as an animal care specialist through a thirty-week program costing around $6,000 in books and fees.

Most certifications are awarded in fields such as welding, nursing, hospice care, computer maintenance and repair, mechanics, and metalworking. Research conducted at the Georgetown Center on Education and the Workforce found that the certificates most sought by people with only high school diplomas include certified nursing assistant, commercial truck driver, and insurance agent, lines of work that currently command annual earnings (on average) of $42,000, $49,000, and $50,000, respectively. And believe it or not, certification programs also exist in high-level, professional fields such as accounting, architecture, aviation, and business.

Some certificates—such as the CMA (certified management accountant) certificate—are awarded by industry organizations. Others are awarded by two- and four-year colleges and universities on either a credit or not-for-credit basis. These postsecondary programs are offered in a vast number of interesting disciplines: aviation, criminal justice and corrections, real estate, tourism, information technology, and dozens more. A growing number are offered online, as well—a great option for those with day jobs or complicated schedules that make it difficult to attend class at appointed times.

As just one example of a college-sponsored program, let's look more closely at the graphic design certificate program offered at Salem State University in Massachusetts, which offers courses in advertising, desktop publishing, corporate art, graphic production, and interactive multimedia. Participants in Salem State's program are required to complete only six core college-level courses and three electives, which allows them to complete their studies in a short period of learning time. These requirements, in other words, are far less extensive and more concentrated on applicable skills than those needed for associate and bachelor's degrees, which is why one team of researchers referred to certificates as "bite-sized awards."[5] In terms of credit hours, our graphic design example requires half the hours and cost of an associate degree and one-fourth the hours and cost of a nonresidential baccalaureate program. And because the requirements are more practical, focused, and concentrated on skills than those needed to earn associate or bachelor's degrees, they turn out graduates ready to jump right into their chosen jobs.[6]

It's easy to see how one of these programs would offer a competitive advantage to any high school grad who is handy with computers but who lacks experience or formal training, or who can't afford or has no desire to spend two years taking all the general and specialty courses required to earn a two-year associate degree. (Though credits earned through a certificate program usually count toward that degree if the person later decides to go back to school.)

And what is the financial payoff? A 2012 study of certificate awards concluded that recipients often receive *higher pay* than do holders of associate degrees and, in some cases, more than some four-year degree recipients. On average, high school graduates with certificates earn 20 percent more than their counterparts with just a high school diploma—about $35,000 versus $29,000.[7] Even when results are pay neutral, according to the report, the individuals holding certificates are more employable.[8] As one might expect, the largest premiums are paid to individuals who earn certificates in their fields of current employment and training and whose fields of employment are already well paid. Thus, someone working in the aviation industry, a generally well-remunerated field, will most likely experience a bigger pay boost from a certificate than will someone working in food service, a lower-wage industry.[9]

When you look at the math, it's perhaps no surprise that more than one million certificates are awarded in the United States each year, and 11 percent of employed U.S. workers point to their occupational certificates as their highest educational achievement and the entrée to the career path they chose.

||||||||||||||||||||||||||||||||||||||||||||||||||||||||||||||||||||||||||||||||||||||||||||||||||||||||

ONE INDUSTRY'S SOLUTION

In early 2011 the Manufacturing Institute, a trade group representing U.S. manufacturers, initiated a "Manufacturing Skills Certification System." Its goal is threefold: to reduce the shortage of skilled labor experienced by 82 percent of member companies, to give hiring managers an objective indication of what prospective employees already know and can do on the job, and to help companies focus their training initiatives more effectively.

These certificates are intended to take some

of the risk and guesswork out of hiring decisions by validating skills that job candidates need to be productive and successful in entry-level manufacturing positions. The institute's certificates are "stackable"—that is, workers can achieve higher and higher levels of validated technical/occupation competency on top of the basic initial certificate. For example, the holder of a basic certificate might take training in safety, quality practices, manufacturing processes, and maintenance that would qualify him or her as a certified production technician. Six months later he might go on to earn higher-level certifications in machining and metalworking, die casting, fabrication, welding, construction, and other specialized areas.

The Manufacturing Institute maintains a list of high schools, community colleges, technical schools, and universities that are educating students to manufacturing industry standards and giving those students opportunities to earn certifications as a standard part of their educational programs.

Certification programs are available for more job categories than you could imagine, and they are easy to find. The U.S. Department of Labor lists more than five thousand of them by general category—such as "Architecture and Engineering"—on its CareerOneStop website at www.careeronestop.org. If you're curious, you can drill down within a category of interest and find dozens if not hundreds of occupational certification programs and the names of their sponsors. For example: Want to be certified as a paralegal who performs many of the same functions as an attorney? Go to the CareerOneStop website to learn about training organizations that run certification programs in this area. Or maybe you're looking into the possibility of becoming certified as a health fitness specialist or a clinical exercise specialist. Go to the Department of Labor site and you'll learn that the American College of Sports Medicine sponsors certification programs in both areas. Another click on their website will take you to a site that has an abundance of useful information and all the details to get you started learning—and earning—more. Plenty more useful websites are listed in the appendix on page 255.

One thing is clear: Certificate programs are an accessible and affordable option for anyone who wants to become both more knowledgeable and more employable in any one of hundreds of fields or professions but lacks the means or desire to enroll in a traditional college. They also appear to stimulate an appetite for continuing your education. Thirty percent of certificate holders go on to obtain associate degrees, and approximately 13 percent follow a course of study leading to a bachelor's degree. Whatever your personal preference may be, one thing is for certain: Professional and occupational certificates open doors and give people opportunities to test out their abilities and interests, knowing they will benefit from the time and effort they put into learning a new skill.

The Power of Associate Degrees

Lucas Griffin is an example of how far and fast an associate degree can take you: literally. At age thirty-four Lucas is a crew chief for Turner Motorsport's GT race cars, an enterprise he joined in 2009 after three years with Newman/Haas Racing. The cars Lucas helps to build and service are at the cutting edge of speed and endurance, and he has followed them and their drivers around North America, Australia, and Europe. The job of a race crew chief is nothing if not challenging.

"The season kicks off with the Daytona twenty-four-hour race," he told me. "That requires weeks of preparation and long days. During the race, our four drivers get rest breaks, but I'm working the entire twenty-four hours." Yet, despite the demands of his job, Lucas wouldn't trade it for anything; he enjoys and is proud of the work he is doing—not to mention the laurels his cars have brought to his team and its owners. He is also doing well financially, earning significantly more than most of his college-educated contemporaries.

That Lucas would someday find his way to an automotive vocation would have surprised many who knew him early on in life. His was a professional family: Both of his parents earned advanced degrees. One grandfather had been a corporate lawyer; the other, an electrical engineer, had been a pioneer in the field of wind energy. Not surprisingly, his parents enrolled Lucas in one of the ten best public high schools in Massachusetts—a school from which most graduates went on to top colleges, including Harvard, Princeton, and Yale.

Luckily for Lucas, despite its emphasis on college preparation, Hamilton-Wenham Regional High School offered a number of excellent shop classes, which he enrolled in and thoroughly enjoyed. "Fab-tec was really good," he remembers. "We learned basic mechanics and welding and built a three-wheel recumbent bicycle." But like many other high schools, Hamilton-Wenham's shop classes were gradually being phased out. So Lucas transferred to a neighboring high school offering more automotive mechanical classes.

Lucas took immediately to this course of study—so much so that, instead of following the normal college pathway after high school like most of his peers, Lucas enrolled in a technical institute in Boston that had a strong focus on engineering and the mechanical arts. A year later he learned that a school called WyoTech, in Laramie, Wyoming, near the Medicine Bow Mountains, had more of the specific courses he wanted, so he transferred there (as a bonus, it was near some of North

America's best ski slopes). A little over a year after arriving at WyoTech, Lucas earned an associate degree in automotive technology. The program gave Lucas access to specialized training in high-performance engines, chassis design and fabrication, welding, machining, metal shaping, and service management that would serve him well in the future—and much sooner than he expected.

Associate degree in hand, Lucas had no trouble finding work as an auto mechanic, and before long he became so well-known as one of the best in the area that he was asked to return to WyoTech—this time as an instructor, teaching chassis fabrication. But the young mechanic was ultimately looking to work someplace more exciting than in a classroom. He'd gone to a lot of Indy and sports car races, and he liked their competitive, high-energy ambience. Eager to be a part of it, he applied for a job with Newman/Haas Racing, a top-drawer, thirty-man team owned by Paul Newman, the late actor and philanthropist, whom Lucas remembers as a "cool guy." He started as a front-end mechanic, then moved up to lead mechanic. At Turner Motorsport, he anticipates becoming a team manager one day.

Life on the race circuit has highs and lows. "When the cars are doing well, it's great," said Lucas. "But when they're not winning or when a driver puts our car into the wall, it's a downer with lots of long days ahead." Still, Lucas couldn't be happier with his career choice. When I last spoke with him, he was in Belgium, helping his team build a new car for the prestigious European racing circuit.

And he got there with just a two-year associate degree, on-the-job training, and a whole lot of grit, determination, and passion for the skills he was building.

"*Every Thing* That Is Useful"

It was not that long ago that most people assumed they would finish high school and then get a job. More recently, the expected career path became that a person would graduate high school, go to college, and *then* get a job. They would stay in their chosen line of work and on their employer's rosters through their working lives, collect a nice pension, and retire in comfort. Well, young people today only have to look at the careers of their parents to know we can't assume that any longer. Owing to changes in the economy, technology, globalization, and the business-employee relationship, finding, losing, and changing jobs many times throughout our working lives has become the new normal. Each new job requires brand-new knowledge and skills. Fortunately, it is easier than ever for workers to stay relevant and attractive to employers by refreshing their skill sets and keeping up to date with new technologies, advancements, and developments in their chosen field. Associate degrees are one of the best places to begin.

An associate degree is an affordable undergraduate

academic degree focused on imparting advanced skills that will increase students' earning potential and provide employment opportunities in some of today's hottest job industries. Though a certification program can sometimes be completed in as little as thirty weeks, an associate degree usually takes two years to complete. There are two types of associate degrees: occupationally focused degrees and transfer degrees. The first integrates the educational elements of traditional college with job-ready skills training that employers value, preparing students to step immediately into the workplace with a substantial set of practical skills. The second type prepares a person to transfer into a bachelor's degree program at a traditional four-year college or university. The cost and credit-hour requirements of the two are roughly equivalent. Since we are talking primarily about alternatives to traditional college, our focus here will be on the former: occupational degree programs.

Like those of secondary vocational education in America, the roots of the American system of community and technical colleges go back to Colonial times. In 1749, Benjamin Franklin published his *Proposals Relating to the Education of Youth in Pensilvania* [*sic*], a document that led to the establishment of the Academy of Philadelphia (later the University of Pennsylvania). In it, Franklin differentiated between what he called "useful" and "ornamental" learning.

"As to their STUDIES," he wrote of the students who would attend the academy, "it would be well if they could be taught *every Thing* that is useful, and every Thing that is ornamental." The "useful" things that Franklin had in mind are today being taught in occupational associate degree programs, where the curriculum is short on Homer and Proust but long on the practical skills that make people job-ready and highly employable.

While vocational and occupational certifications add muscle to the high school diploma and are an affordable and next-step option for high school graduates interested in pursuing a skills-based work life, it could be a good idea to take your education a step further and pursue an associate degree. Why? While many followers of the CTE path have done well over the span of their careers either by rising through the ranks of their companies or through self-employment or small business ownership, there's no denying that those whose education stops with a high school diploma—even those with additional professional certifications—may encounter obstacles without additional academic classroom education. The Center on Education and Workforce at Georgetown University estimates that in 2020, two of every three jobs will require some form of postsecondary education.[1] And as globalization and computer-driven automation continue to squeeze more and more lower-skilled jobs out of the economy, life is likely to become more challenging for those without any kind of postsecondary education in the years ahead. So while skills-based certificates are one solid solution for high school graduates who are ready and anxious to land a job, occupationally oriented associate degrees can give you a competitive edge on certificate holders in the job market and broaden the range of jobs, positions, and future levels of professional advancement.

Over the last several decades associate degrees have become an increasingly attractive option for high school grads and others who want a more formal educational environment without the high cost of an on-campus living experience. You can earn them throughout the United States in community, junior, or technical colleges, and even some four-year colleges and universities, and in a wide range of skill areas, including aviation, computer technology, biomedical design and manufacturing, paralegal studies, nursing, hospitality management, sustainable horticulture, advanced manufacturing, mechatronics, and dozens more. The cost of a two-year associate degree in the United States—tuition and fees—averages about $6,300, according to research by the College Board,[2] putting it within the financial reach and comfort level of most students and families. By comparison, that same study pegged in-state tuition and fees for four-year bachelor's degree programs at public institutions at roughly $34,000, and $116,000 at private institutions. Or, put another way, on average, the cost of tuition and fees at U.S. community colleges is only 36 percent of the tuition costs incurred at four-year colleges. So for a young person who wants more education but is not enthusiastic or ready to take on the commitment—or the cost—of a four-year program, an associate degree offers the perfect opportunity to continue learning job-ready skills while acquiring a higher educational credential—and a leg up in the job market.

||||||||||||||||||||||||||||||||||||||||||||||||||||||||||||||||||||||||||||||||||||||||||||||||||||||||||||||||||||||||||||||||||||||||||

WHY COMMUNITY COLLEGE?

Nearly 12.8 million students are enrolled in America's 1,100 community colleges and postsecondary tech schools; a number that represents 44 percent of all undergraduates.[3] Forty-five percent of them are ethnic or racial minorities, and two-thirds of the 12.8 million attend part-time. The average age of community college students is 28; more than half of them work as they attend school.

As a financial investment, a two-year college education has a high average return—much higher than the long-term return of the stock market. A study done at Ivy Tech Community College reported that students who completed professional certifications or associate degree programs more than doubled their earning power, achieving on average $5.10 in higher future wages for every $1 they invested in their schooling.[4]

What fields of study are occupational-oriented two-year-college undergraduates in the United States studying? Here is the distribution that stabilized since the 2007–8 academic year:

Field of Study	Percentage of Degree/ Credential-Seeking Students
Health science	39.8%
Manufacturing, construction, repair, and transportation	6.8%
Business and marketing	25.3%
Engineering and architecture	8.5%
Consumer services	7.4%
Protective services	7.3%
Computer and information sciences	6.9%

Source: CTE Statistics, National Center for Educational Statistics, http://nces.ed.gov/surveys/ctes/tables/P43.asp.

Perhaps you wonder whether occupational associate degree holders enjoy the earnings and career benefits of those with four-year college degrees. The answer is a resounding yes. While it's true that students who successfully complete their bachelor's degree can earn more than those with only an associate's degree, remember that many students who enter a four-year degree program don't complete it. Moreover, research shows that many associate degree holders enjoy *better* employment prospects than their collegiate counterparts, and a full one-third of them start their careers at higher pay levels. A growing number of college graduates are discovering this fact, as they find themselves working in low-paid positions for which their costly degrees were not needed: as baristas, waiters, shopping mall retail clerks, and so forth. You may be one of them. Your son, daughter, niece, or nephew may be another.

Occupational associate degree holders also command a wage premium over peers who have earned associate degrees in nonoccupational fields: on average $9,000 more per year. And if the associate degree is in a high-demand field such as health care, he or she can earn an average annual wage premium of almost $20,000.

Just as with some high school vocational education programs, occupational associate degree programs are usually designed with the needs of local employers and industries in mind, and offer students the opportunity for plenty of hands-on experience, often through cooperative arrangements with companies. This is a pathway to higher employability and earnings, and a huge advantage when answering the inevitable "What experience do you have?" interview question.

To get a sense of the employment opportunities and wages available to associate degree holders, consider this small example set, which I've taken from the U.S. Bureau of Labor Statistics online *Occupational Handbook Outlook*. An associate degree can lead to each one of these rewarding and highly respectable careers.

Median Earning by Educational Achievement
(Through Associate Degree, Age Twenty-Five and Higher)

Health Care	
Cardiovascular technologists and technicians and vascular technologists. Cardiovascular technologists and technicians and vascular technologists use imaging technology to help physicians diagnose cardiac (heart) and peripheral vascular (blood vessel) ailments in patients. They also help physicians treat problems with cardiac and vascular systems, such as blood clots.	$60,350 per year $29.02 per hour
Dental hygienists. Dental hygienists clean teeth, examine patients for oral diseases such as gingivitis, and provide other preventive dental care. They also educate patients on ways to improve and maintain good oral health.	$70,210 per year $33.75 per hour
Medical laboratory technologists and technicians. These individuals collect samples and perform tests to analyze body fluids, tissue, and other substances.	$47,820 per year $22.99 per hour
Veterinarian technician. Vet techs perform medical tests under the supervision of licensed veterinarians and help veterinarians diagnose the illnesses and injuries of animals.	$30,290 per year $14.56 per hour
Industrial	
Mechanical engineering technician. They help mechanical engineers design, develop, test, and manufacture industrial machinery, consumer products, and other equipment. They may make sketches and rough layouts, record and analyze data, make calculations and estimates, and report their findings. Mechanical engineering technicians may also help with manufacturing processes on the shop floor or with development phases in research and development labs before manufacturing takes place.	$51,980 per year $24.99 per hour

Electro-mechanical technician. Sometimes called "mechatronic" technicians, these cross-disciplinary workers combine knowledge of mechanical technology with knowledge of electrical and electronic circuits. They install, troubleshoot, repair, and upgrade electronic and computer-controlled mechanical systems, such as robotic assembly machines.	$51,820 per year $24.91 per hour
Legal	
Paralegals and legal assistants. Paralegals and legal assistants perform a variety of tasks to support lawyers, including maintaining and organizing files, conducting legal research, and drafting documents.	$46,990 per year $22.59 per hour

Source: U.S. Census Bureau

Two things are worth noting about the occupations listed in the chart above. First is that these fields offer highly respected career opportunities that many in the "college for everyone" camp might not recognize as an option for a graduate of an associate program or a community college. Second is the diversity of careers represented, with job descriptions ranging from building robots to caring for sick or injured animals to crafting legal arguments to treating critically ill patients.

Of course, an associate degree is not necessarily the end of the line in terms of education—or earning power. Transfer degrees—associate degrees that prepare students to transfer into baccalaureate and even graduate programs—can have great value as well. Twenty-seven percent of U.S. baccalaureate degree holders in recent years, in fact, have come up through the community college system.

Combined with a bachelor's degree, a community college associate degree in a health care, IT, manufacturing, or other high-demand area can be a winning proposition, especially for recipients who get some on-the-job experience as part of their studies. These people's résumés really stand out to employers, who see them as skilled individuals who can be productive from day one—and with degrees to boot.

The number of college grads currently following this pathway is significant in today's job market, and it's easy to see why. One anonymous comment to a blog on this subject put it this way: "Upon graduating with my BA in English with no desire to teach and no money for law school, I found myself at the CC [community college] to get a paralegal degree so that I could get a 'real' job." This individual is part of a growing class of students that educators call "reverse transfers." In the past, a reverse transfer was a student who had dropped back from a four-year college to a two-year institution—someone who may have followed the four-year college route for a semester or two, then become disenchanted, or run out of money. Today, reverse transfers include a growing number of four-year college graduates who then follow that up by enrolling into an associate degree program, either because it offers the career option they "really" wanted or simply because they have discovered the value in fortifying their academic-oriented résumés with real-world training.

Like occupational certificates, associate degrees aren't just for recent high school graduates or young people;

anyone can attain one at any point in their career. In fact, many students in associate programs are in their twenties or thirties and have many years in the workforce under their belts—further evidence for the anti-trackers that going straight from high school into the workforce far from precludes continuing one's education later.

Picture Your Success in Diagnostic Imaging

Diagnostic imaging is a multibillion-dollar global business and a key element in today's health care landscape. A field dedicated to the early detection and diagnosis of diseases using magnetic resonance imaging, CT scanners, ultrasound technology, and X-rays, this is an industry that relies upon a workforce highly trained in the specialized skills required to run and operate complex machines. From the technologists who operate the imaging devices, to the field engineers who install, repair, and maintain them, to those who sell the equipment to hospitals and clinics, a career in this field can be both fulfilling as well as financially rewarding.

Just ask Paul Pfiffer, who enjoys a challenging and well-paid career as a product sales manager for a leading health care equipment manufacturer. Like many of the other individuals we've met throughout this book, Paul didn't follow the traditional high school to four-year college route. Although he certainly had the knowledge and technical aptitude to attend college right after high school, due to family priorities, he entered the military, where he became a communications equipment technician with the hopes the training would prepare him for a similar career after his service was complete. When it didn't, Paul took a job to pay the bills while he attempted to break into a career in the electronics industry. After the company that hired him closed down, Paul decided to take advantage of the educational assistance the company was offering its displaced workers and enrolled in an accelerated associate degree program that focused on practical hands-on electronic training. Two years later, within just a week of graduation, he had landed an entry-level position with a small manufacturer of MRI surface coils. Paul told me, "I was not afraid to take this entry-level position as I saw it as a stepping-stone into an organization where there appeared to be opportunities for growth." And he was right.

Paul's experience, education, and determination soon earned him a promotion to the role of engineering lab manager, where he led several teams, built client relationships, and conducted field-based research and product testing on clients' scanners. That experience led him to General Electric, where he decided to add yet another skill to his skill set: sales. He recalls, "most of my counterparts at the time were bright four-year college graduates; however, most lacked real-world experience, so after establishing myself within the organization I charted out my new pathway by taking a role within the company's internal sales channel." But his education didn't end there. A lifelong learner, Paul took advantage of GE's in-house training programs to expand his knowledge of his product, his field, and frontline customer service. He was soon selected as the team's MRI product champion, and ultimately offered the role of operations manager for the twenty-member team. This paved the way for yet another opportunity: a transition into outside sales as an account executive, a product sales specialist, and eventually into sales leadership. Today Paul manages a sales team of product sales specialists in the billion-dollar growth market of X-ray equipment with Siemens Healthcare USA. Firmly established as a knowledgeable, versatile executive in an in-demand, stable industry, he enjoys a rewarding and well-compensated work life.

And what do I mean by "well compensated"? I polled several companies in medical imaging and discovered the market rate for a technologist is anywhere from $40,000 to $90,000; a field engineer from $70,000 to $100,000; and salesperson anywhere from $85,000 to $175,000 per year.

If you think a two-year associate degree program might be the route for you, do your homework and be sure to ask the admissions and recruiting counselors some, if not all, of the following questions:

- What is the typical wage paid to degree holders in the occupational field that interests you? Remember, compensation varies widely between occupations. The *Occupational Outlook Hand-*

book from the U.S. Bureau of Labor Statistics is a great guide: www.bls.gov/ooh/.

- What is the labor market demand for the occupational skill you aim to develop? Apart from the *Occupational Outlook Handbook,* you can research which local employers are hiring and then cross-reference a college course catalog to see if the courses offered match the skills employers need.

- Does the school you are considering have close ties to area employers? Which ones? The best schools have close ties with local employers *and* are synchronized with the actual local demand. To start, you'll want to find out if local employers advise on curriculum, and whether they sponsor work-study programs. As an example of one such program, Vigor Industrial, the Oregon shipbuilder mentioned in the previous chapter, opened a training center in partnership with South Seattle Community College within its Harbor Island shipyard in 2013. The facility includes a computer lab, classroom space, and an industrial training floor with welding booths and machining equipment. There, students get a preview of the work and work environment, an opportunity to apply what they've learned in class, and practical tips from regular employees. A strong employer-school link like that is your best guarantee that the job you want will be there after two years of study, and that your instruction will match the real needs of a prospective employer. So go to the school's website or call their admissions office or career centers to find out if they offer any work-study or apprenticeship programs with nearby companies. You might even check faculty rosters to see if instructors in the areas you want to study hail from or have ties with local companies. Even if this doesn't lead directly to a position post-graduation, these are always good connections to have—and who knows? The relationship may open the door to an exciting opportunity later on your career path.

- If the program is offered through a community college, you can also check the institution's overall ranking at a website such as www.collegemeasures.org.

COMMUNITY COLLEGE STANDOUTS

It can't be denied that in many circles community college degrees lack the prestige associated with degrees from traditional universities. But this is a wholly unfair perception. In fact, one of the (unfortunately) best-kept secrets in our society is how many of our most revered cultural icons are actually products of the community college system. Luckily the lingering stigma hasn't prevented thousands of these community college alumni from accomplishing great things in a wide range of industries and professions. Here are just a few notable people who have.

George Lucas. Award-winning filmmaker and creator of such classic films as *Star Wars*, *Indiana Jones*, and many others.

Eileen Collins. Legendary NASA astronaut and the first female pilot and commander of a space shuttle.

Frank Gehry. Internationally acclaimed architect.

Nolan Ryan. Baseball Hall of Famer and former president of the Texas Rangers.

Dr. Craig Venter. National Medal of Science honoree; biologist and pioneer in human gene sequencing.

Gwendolyn Brooks. Pulitzer Prize winner and former U.S. poet laureate.

Billy Crystal. Emmy and Tony Award–winning comedian, actor, and director.

Nolan Archibald. CEO/chairman of the Stanley Black & Decker Corporation.

Jim Lehrer. Legendary journalist, news anchor, and novelist.

Sam Shepard. Pulitzer Prize–winning play-
wright and film director.

Ross Perot. Billionaire industrialist and former
presidential candidate.

Tom Hanks. Oscar-winning actor.

So far we've discussed how the certificate programs
and occupational associate degrees from two-year colleges are quick and affordable ways to boost employability and earning power, and how many types of people can
benefit from them: high school grads who need a résumé
boost, unemployed and *under*employed college graduates
whose degrees haven't opened the right doors, middle-
aged workers displaced by outsourcing, and gainfully
employed people who want to advance in their current
careers.

This brings us to apprenticeships, yet another alternative career pathway that provides incredible opportunities
for rebooting your skill set and gaining practical work
experience at any stage in your life or career.

A program in which a protégé learns hands-on skills
in the workplace under the direct supervision of a fully
skilled person, the apprenticeship is the Western world's
oldest form of occupational training, and this nation's
history is chock-full of examples of great men who became master craftsmen, artisans, inventors, and even
statesmen by following this track. Today, modern apprenticeship programs confer arguably even more advantages

and opportunities than the programs described in this and the last chapter. The benefits of modern apprenticeships are so many for learners, employers, and the public coffers alike that I've devoted the next chapter to them. Whether you are a student, a parent, an employer, or a policy maker, I urge you to turn the page and read on.

5

The Magic of Apprenticeships

When you find yourself making a presentation to a large group of people, it's generally a good sign when audience members nod enthusiastically as you speak. It is especially rewarding when you find yourself talking to a room of men and women from all over the world who are intently interested in the subject about which you are most passionate: in my case, skills and apprenticeships. So I'll admit to having been slightly deflated when, on one such occasion, I wrapped up the session and took the first question from a lady in the third row, who excitedly asked, "You work for Donald Trump, right? You know, from the show *The Apprentice*?" From that day on, to avoid any confusion with the popular TV show, I like to kick off my talks by describing what the term "apprenticeship" means to me.

Although there are many subtly different meanings of the word, and terminology differs country to country, for most businesses and organizations and around the world—Donald Trump's definition notwithstanding—an apprenticeship is best described as any program that offers its participants the opportunity to master an occupational area and learn hands-on skills under the direct supervision of a skilled expert in a specific field or craft. Such programs offer a host of benefits that complement if not exceed those of certifications and two-year associate degrees.

As I've mentioned, my own apprenticeship experience—undertaken at the point in my life where everyone was recommending attending college—helped shape my life in many positive ways; I am living, breathing proof of the power of the apprenticeship as the launch pad and pathway to a successful and fulfilling career.

My years as an apprentice chef were not only some of the most exciting and rewarding of my career, but they also equipped me with the structure, skills, confidence, and financial independence to pursue opportunities that got me to where I am today. But that's not the only reason I am such a firm believer that apprenticeships are one of the most powerful educational tools we have in closing the jobs-skills gap in America and elsewhere. My work designing frontline skills programs and matching employees and employers has afforded me access to firsthand evidence proving beyond a shadow of a doubt that apprenticeships give people the opportunity to learn the skills that will position them for gainful employment. They also provide companies with a ready and able pool of skilled, job-ready *workers who have been trained in the precise competencies and skills that are needed for a company, a country, and an economy to grow.* I would go so far as to call apprenticeships our best weapon in the war to reduce unemployment, rebuild the middle class, and restore America's status as a leader on a global economic scale.

Apprentices are essentially employees who are paid while they learn, both in the workplace and in more traditional educational environments. In many countries, apprentices are encouraged to take classes within the public education system, and often tuition assistance is offered and fees are subsidized.

Although on-the-job learning offers the apprentice a huge competitive advantage in the job market, the real added value (or, as the chef in me would say, the key ingredient) of an apprenticeship program is the unique and potentially life-changing one-on-one relationship between protégé and mentor it offers. This professional relationship is far more personal and less formal than the one usually found between professor and student in a lecture-style setting where the class size can number anywhere from thirty to three hundred, and the course is often taught by a graduate student, teaching assistant, or one of a revolving door of adjunct professors. Instead of spending a semester or entire academic year listening to ninety-minute lectures two or three times a week, an apprentice has daily one-on-one interactions with supervisors, colleagues, and peers who truly challenge and inspire them. More often than not, apprentices find themselves engaged in a constant back-and-forth exchange that involves diagnosing problems, forming opinions, and collaborating on solutions.

The skills, knowledge, and problem-solving abilities gleaned through these exchanges are a big part of why, in one UK study, employers ranked their apprentices as the most employable of their young people—even above those with college degrees.[1] The opportunity to develop multiple professional relationships at an early stage in their working lives is often identified as a key factor for former apprentices' career success later on. Some of these apprenticeship relationships can last a lifetime; talented and accomplished people in your social network can still open doors for you five, ten, or even twenty years down the road. I know for me, being in the trenches with so many talented people forged bonds that have lasted decades; I still count some of the people I met during my apprentice years as my closest friends and most trusted colleagues and sounding boards today. Oh, and let's not forget, apprenticeships foster an intergenerational collaboration that can impart a level of maturity, self-confidence, and understanding of the world that is often lacking in the structured confines of a campus setting.

The Harvard "Pathways to Prosperity" report of 2011 described it this way:

> The most intensive forms of workplace learning—apprenticeship and sustained internships—are especially effective in meeting the developmental needs of young people. They provide a structure to support the transition from adolescence to adulthood lacking for the majority of young

people in the U.S. Apprenticeships provide increasingly demanding responsibilities and challenges in an intergenerational work setting that lends a structure to each day. Adult relationships are built on support and accountability, mentoring and supervision.

Add to that the opportunity to learn skills and principles that directly relate to the task in front of them and to gain, early on in their career, the values and life lessons that will benefit them throughout their work life, and you can understand why many young people and adults would prefer this real-world classroom to the more traditional kind.

Keep in mind that, just like associate degrees and professional certificates, apprenticeships are not just educational opportunities for young people or recent college graduates; they are viable options for people of any age. One of the most successful apprentices I know started her apprenticeship at age thirty-nine as a heavy vehicle mechanic. Gayleen was raised on a remote island, where she was one of twelve children. From an early age, she loved watching her oldest brother, an outboard marine mechanic, strip down marine motors in the backyard. An opportunity to start an apprenticeship didn't present itself till her late thirties. And she is not alone. In Australia, for instance, 42 percent of apprentices are over the age of twenty-five, and it's not unusual to meet apprentices in their forties or fifties.

The point is that no matter your age, an apprentice-ship offers a collaborative, real-world learning opportunity between an employee, an employer, and an educational/training provider. It is a unique learning relationship—one in which the apprentice progressively gains knowledge, occupational mastery, and confidence while contributing an increasing level of value to the employer.

Today, apprenticeships are experiencing a resurgence. Educators, business leaders, and government officials are increasingly recognizing the vital role they play in transi-tioning people from school to work.

In this chapter I'll introduce you to some amazing people from all corners of the world who feel as strongly as I do about the value of apprenticeships. You'll learn about the rich history of apprenticeships, as well as the promise they hold for future generations. And you will meet some aspiring apprentices working in fields many millionaires would pay to spend a day in.

Duxford Aerodrome, Cambridgeshire, England

Seventy-five years ago, during the desperately fought Bat-tle of Britain at the beginning of World War II, squad-rons of Supermarine Spitfires roared off from Duxford to defend English airspace against fierce attack. Today, the country faces a very different threat: high youth unemployment. And once again the venerable Spitfire may play a critical role in its rescue.

The British-built Spitfire, a plane known for its high performance, was a frontline aircraft used by Britain's Royal Air Force Fighter Command during the Second World War. Although more than twenty-two thousand Spitfires and Seafires (the naval version) were built between 1938 and 1946, only a few hundred have survived. Fewer still are flyable. Prized by private collectors, especially in the United States, restored Spitfires and other vintage war-birds can fetch upward of $4 million. So it's no surprise that in the late 1980s the Aircraft Restoration Company was founded to meet that demand and to save the iconic Spitfire and its brethren from the dustbin of history. Since that founding more than twenty-five years ago, ARC has restored and maintained dozens of British Spitfires and Hurricanes, German Me109s, American P-51 Mustangs and B-25 Mitchell bombers, and many more; chances are that you've seen one or another of these aircraft at air shows or in movies such as *Memphis Belle* or *Battle of Britain*. But what's most impressive about ARC in the context of our discussion isn't its credits on the silver screen; it's the company's gold standard apprenticeship program.

After learning about the company and its renowned employee apprenticeship program, I was able to arrange a visit with ARC's founder and leader, John Romain, who I hoped would be able to provide insight on the secret ingredient to the program's success.

Entering Duxford airfield, an hour north of London, is like entering another world. At the guardhouse, I was directed through a village of hangars housing one of the world's largest collections of modern and vintage aircraft. Duxford is home to the Imperial War Museum. "Turn left at the B-17 Flying Fortress," the guard told me. "Then take a right past the Concorde. Then drive down the airstrip two hundred yards."

Here I met John Romain, a former Hawker Siddeley and British Aerospace engineer and a highly experienced warbird pilot. A fit man in his fifties with touches of gray sprinkled throughout his no-nonsense haircut, John met me in a zippered flight suit. The man seemed at home at the airfield amid hangars that shelter dozens of planes, including Spitfires in various stages of restoration. He's clearly passionate about flying and about the rare planes he and his team bring back to life.

John is passionate not only about rebuilding planes at ARC but also about skills development in the British aviation industry. Apprentices are an important element of his plan—so important that his own son seized the opportunity to sign on as an apprentice at his father's enterprise. "Apprenticeships are critical not only to the survival of my own company but to the aircraft industry," John said. "I need a skilled workforce to take my company forward."

After giving me a look around the machine shop, paint-spraying booth, and other areas geared to bring old war fighters back to life, John introduced me to Mark

Parr, a lead engineer and a guy with an obvious passion for the detailed work that goes into restoring these old planes. Mark's infatuation with airplanes began around age six, when his heart would race every time he heard the roar of Spitfires at air shows and watched their sleek gray outlines slice through the sky. At seventeen, he began a sheet metal apprenticeship at a major aerospace company, where he was eventually placed in a full-time position and where he continued to progress rapidly through the ranks. Mark recalls the day when the company phoned him with an offer to join ARC. "I said, 'So I get to work with Spitfires—and I get paid? Wow!'"

Mark signed on with a team that brought a passion for excellence, a respect for history, and a multitude of aptitudes and trades under one roof: sheet metal workers, engine mechanics, airframe fitters, electricians, riveters, spray painters, machinists, and even woodworkers (many vintage planes had wooden parts). Most team members were multiskilled, and all had a level of creativity and persistence that's essential in this kind of craft, where so many parts have been out of stock for decades and must either be found through detective work, recovered from old crash sites, or fabricated from scratch. Whether aircraft parts are recovered, restored, or handmade, ARC's goal is perfection, and perfection requires craftsmen with high skills and high standards. It was clear from Mark's telling that ARC is a place where the word "skilled" has tangible meaning. Landing a job at ARC can be an ambitious young person's dream come true.

Apprenticeships are a decades-old tradition at the company. Some of the workers I met at Duxford had completed their apprenticeships thirty or so years earlier within the aeronautical industry. The oldest and most experienced of the bunch is "Smudge," a seventy-five-year-old ex-RAF engineer, who, as Mark likes to joke, "did his apprenticeship under the Wright Brothers!" The age issue, however, is no joke. ARC's old-timers are concerned about the know-how of their trade being lost if too few young men and women follow in their footsteps, which is why the company continues to take on new apprentices. The original-apprentices-now-turned-masters are embracing the role of mentors to the next generation of restorers of these iconic aircraft. "The old skills have begun to die off," John told me, "so we started training mechanical and trades engineers ourselves. It is critical to our business. It will give us engineers for the future who have the right skills."

ARC's modern apprenticeship program, now in its eleventh year, mirrors one developed by the British aviation firm de Havilland (now part of BAE Systems) that was once regarded as the best in the world. The secret to their success? There is no question that the thoughtful recruiting of passionate people with a can-do approach gives the program a head start. Add to this the one-on-one skills training the apprentices receive from the business's technical specialists, and John's rock-solid commitment to skills development, and you have a winning formula.

The company's current challenge is to sift through its

many apprenticeship applicants for the handful who are truly committed, have a strong work ethic, and who will hold themselves to very high standards. Attitude and interest trump current skills in this selection process. "We can teach them the technical skills they need," as one apprentice supervisor put it.

On my visit to the facility, I had a chance to observe some of the young apprentices at work. One of them, Steve Wood, or "Woody," started with the company as an apprentice eleven years ago at age sixteen. Like many young people, he disliked sitting in a classroom; he wanted to work with his hands. Now twenty-seven, Woody is an aircraft fitter and supervisor of ARC's current crop of apprentices. "When they first show up they don't know what a spanner is," he told me. "Gradually, though, they're able to complete technical tasks by themselves. Watching that happen is very satisfying." Woody is an example of the power of an apprenticeship to harness a person's passion and sense of purpose, transforming them over time into a master prepared to pass on specialized skills to the next generation.

Watching Woody at work with his young charges reminded me of Bruce, a master chef I worked under as an apprentice chef at the five-star-rated Regent Hotel. Bruce taught us the workings of the kitchen but expected us to learn much more; he understood the customers, their expectations, and what was happening in every part of the hotel. He expected no less from us. Working with him taught me that technical skill is only one piece of what it takes to excel in the work world, and that helped me immensely as my career progressed from cooking to hospitality management to other business ventures. I could see that Mark and Woody's apprentices were being taught similar lessons that would serve them well as they grew in their jobs and took on greater responsibilities in the business. But these apprentices are getting something even more satisfying: a chance to rescue an integral contributor to what Winston Churchill called their nation's "finest hour." And it doesn't hurt that they get to ride in the old warbirds with John and other pilots every so often when finished planes are delivered to a collector in the United States. Once a newly restored aircraft completes a series of flight tests, it is carefully disassembled, packed into crates, and shipped off across the Atlantic. A team of ARC engineers and apprentices fly over to meet and reassemble it for John's final flight check and delivery to the lucky owner. Now that is a business trip we all would like to take!

Interestingly, it is rare to meet anyone who reports having had anything but a positive apprenticeship experience in any field; in fact, research conducted in the United Kingdom in 2013 found that 88 percent of the apprentices surveyed were satisfied with the experience and 78 percent would speak highly of their programs to others. Moreover, some 83 percent claimed that their career prospects had improved as a consequence of their training.[2]

Just as I did as a young man, these ARC apprentices

are learning new work skills every day, gaining more and more confidence, and earning a steady paycheck to boot!

"One If by Land . . ."

What did Paul Revere do before taking the midnight ride to Concord and Lexington? Or Ben Franklin before becoming one of the world's great inventors? Were they lawyers? Statesmen? Did they own businesses? None of the above; Paul was an apprentice to a silversmith, Ben apprenticed to be a printer. And if you happen to drive a Ford, you might be interested to know that Henry Ford, the man who revolutionized the auto industry and founded the Ford Motor Company in 1903, started his career not in the classroom but as an apprentice machinist.

To understand the opportunities apprenticeships offer for today's work world, it is important to step back and look at history. The apprenticeship program under way at Duxford today carries forward the traditions of vocational training that became commonplace in Europe as early as the late Middle Ages, when labor became more specialized as more and more people migrated from the countryside into towns. Apprenticeships during that period fell under the supervision of local guilds and town governments and included blacksmiths, housewrights, bakers, roof thatchers, masons, glazers, cordwainers, barrel makers, brewers, weavers, and clockmakers—to name just a few. Young protégés in those days were known as "prentices."

WHERE DOES THE WORD "APPRENTICE" COME FROM?

The English word *apprentice* has a Latin root: *ap-prehendere*, "to grasp or seize." It likely entered the vocabulary via the Old French term *aprentis*, "someone learning." The modern Spanish term *aprender*, "to learn," derives from the same Latin root.

The apprenticeship systems of Europe traveled to North America with Colonial immigration and, until the early nineteenth century, were an important mechanism of mainstream education. Though some apprenticeships were informal, most involved a voluntary contractual period of indenture in which both apprentice and master had rights and obligations. In general, the apprentice would agree to work without pay for the term of the contract, and promise to keep trade secrets and generally stay out of trouble. For his part, the master agreed to provide room and board, train the apprentice in his craft, and often teach him to read, write, and do simple arithmetic.

Apprentices of the preindustrial period lived under their masters' roofs and worked in their homes and shops. Once they completed their term of learning and service, apprentices, now granted the title of *journeymen*, would travel town to town, selling their services for a day's pay. A few years of applied work and evidence of skill would then qualify the journeyman for the title of *master* from the relevant guild, which entitled them to set up a permanent workshop and have apprentices of their own. Today in many trades these craftsmen and -women are still known as apprentice masters.

While apprenticeship systems in northern Europe remained strong through the twentieth century and continue to be strong today, their counterparts in North America began to decline as the notion of indentureship became politically unacceptable, and as the rise of free public education offered an alternative path to economic betterment. The tradition of apprentices living with their masters also went out of favor at this time, and modest wages took the place of room and board in apprenticeship contracts.

Not surprisingly, the industrial revolution dealt a blow to the apprenticeship system in the United States. Once assembly lines and factories made it easy to mass-produce items exponentially faster than through the old by-hand methods, many apprenticeships and the crafts they trained for evaporated.

But while many *craft* apprenticeships disappeared, new types of apprenticeships emerged in the era of mass production. The industrial age created a demand for machinists, electrical workers, metalworkers, plumbers, equipment maintenance specialists, and more—each of which required specialized skills that took years to master. Thus a new system for training workers in these hands-on skills emerged—one that is not unlike the model of apprenticeship that persists today.

From the industrial revolution up until the mid-twentieth century most apprenticeships were found in manufacturing, the building trades, and the utilities industries. In the decades since, they have expanded into other fields: health and public safety, information technology, and food and hospitality. Today, companies in industries ranging from advanced aeronautics to financial services have implemented apprenticeship programs. In 2013, even UPS, the giant express delivery enterprise, joined the list with its own program. What these diverse companies have in common is the need to "skill up" as they compete in the ever-changing global economy.

The U.S. Labor Department's Office of Apprenticeship continues to expand the range of apprenticeship offerings available in response to the changing needs of employers. But at the same time, the number of registered apprentices in the U.S. population has been steadily declining. As you can see on the graph below, the number of people in registered apprenticeships dropped from roughly 470,000 in 2002 to around 287,000 in 2013. Globalization and other economic forces including the financial crisis have driven this decline, particularly in industries like construction. Many companies took jobs offshore.

Number of Active Registered U.S. Apprentices and Programs (in Thousands)

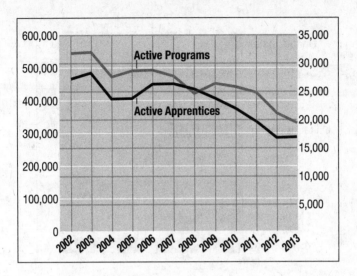

Source: U.S. Department of Labor, www.doleta.gov/oa/
data_statistics.cfm.

The decline of manufacturing jobs contributed to the drop as well. However, the "college for everyone" doctrine and resulting stigma against skilled labor have likely marginalized apprenticeship in the U.S. economy. The unfortunate result of this confluence of forces is that less than 1 percent of U.S. workers enroll in apprenticeship programs today—a tiny fraction of what we find in northern European countries, the United Kingdom, and Australia, where apprentices generally constitute a much larger percentage of the working population.

While the number of U.S. apprentices and programs

Apprentices in Major Developed Countries

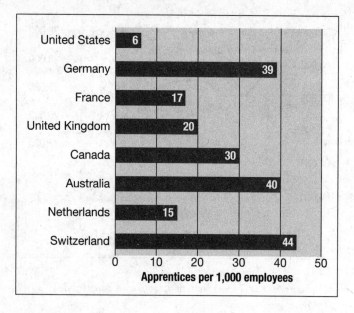

is in decline, the reverse is true in the United Kingdom, where there were 510,000 new apprenticeship commencements in 2013. It's interesting to note that 45 percent of these were apprentices twenty-five years of age or older, and 55 percent were female—quite a shift in a tradition that used to attract mostly young males. Indeed, one reason for the increase in these numbers in the United Kingdom is the extension of apprenticeships into industries and occupations often dominated by women. For example, you can now do an apprenticeship in public health and social care, plant nursery, and child care.

Despite the decline in their numbers, there is a new effort by the federal government to turn the tide. In June

2014, on the heels of President Obama's announcement of a $100 million grant program and a four-year $2 billion budget proposal aimed at doubling the number of apprenticeships in the country, Secretary of Labor Thomas Perez spoke to a group of international experts from the United Kingdom, South Africa, and Australia, as well as local stakeholders including government officials, educators, and program managers. Secretary Perez spoke with passion and commitment, telling the audience at the Urban Institute in Washington about the "huge and bright future" he sees for apprenticeships in the coming years.

"Over the last few decades, we have somehow underinvested in the area of apprenticeship; we have undervalued, underappreciated, and underutilized apprentices' look at the global context." He remarked, "[Yet] apprenticeships provide a spectacular return on investment for everybody involved: labor, management, and government. For every tax payer dollar we spend on apprenticeship we see twenty-seven dollars in benefits.

"I talk to way too many parents and I tell them that apprenticeship is a great opportunity, and they say no, no, no my kid is going to college because they have a misconception about what apprenticeship is. Apprenticeship . . . enables you to get on the higher ed. superhighway with on ramps and off ramps that will allow you to move flexibly up the ladder. These are programs that allow you to get the skills of the twenty-first century and punch your ticket to the middle class."

Another bright spot is the United Services Military

Apprenticeship Program (USMAP), which offers members of the navy, coast guard, and marine corps opportunities to improve their job skills and complete civilian apprenticeship requirements while on active duty. Active apprentices in USMAP grew from 51,645 in 2008 to 87,675 in 2013.[3] Another quality program is run by the International Brotherhood of Electrical Workers, a labor union founded in 1891 that represents workers in the electrical industry and other related fields.

To see this program in action, I decided to visit the modern, well-equipped training center operated by the IBEW Local 26 in Lanham, Maryland, less than an hour by car from the heart of Washington, D.C. One of the center's assistant directors, Ralph Neidert, was kind enough to give me a tour of the facility. Ralph is a serious, no-nonsense guy, and he clearly runs a tight ship: valuable traits in a field where a mistake can be dangerous and costly.

The IBEW's five-year apprenticeship program is among the most thorough I've encountered. Lanham's current nine hundred participants must complete eight hundred hours of classroom instruction combined with another eight thousand hours of on-the-job training under supervision. During the first three years, apprentices are taught elements of the trade that are common to all electrical specialties and ones that, according to Ralph, haven't changed for a hundred years. To underscore that point, he showed me two side-by-side photos of apprentice training classes: one from the 1950s and another, shot from the same angle and in a similar classroom, from just a few years ago. In the first photo, an instructor stands at a blackboard explaining an electrical concept. In the more recent photo, the instructor is explaining the very same concept, except at a whiteboard. The lessons written on these boards are identical. Once that three-year core is mastered, apprentices undergo two more years of training in whichever specialized sector of the electrical trade they wish to pursue on the job: photovoltaic installations, industrial power, building automation, residential wiring, or one of the myriad other options.

This is hands-on learning at its best. Most of the center's classrooms feature "live" replicas of the electrical apparatuses that apprentices will encounter in the field: breaker boxes, wired outlets, alarm and building control systems, and so forth. Students practice what they learn in large-group lectures on these various fixtures and systems under the supervision of instructors, usually in a ten-to-one student-to-teacher ratio.

And the Lanham training center does more than teach technical skills. It helps its apprentices find employment, both during their years of study and afterward, acting both as a register of available jobs and a career center that does its best to see that its members are properly placed. It also maintains standards with a three-strikes policy. Any apprentice who receives more than three employer complaints—about workmanship or punctuality—is asked to leave the program.

U.S. Apprenticeship Quick Statistics

3 million	Number of annual graduates from U.S. high schools
125,000	Number of U.S. apprenticeship positions open annually
30% to 70%	Percent of young people in non-U.S. high-income countries who enter apprenticeship training
3% to 5%	Estimated percent of young people in the United States who enter apprenticeship training (registered and unregistered)
22,000	Number of U.S. companies currently offering apprenticeships
$25 million to $40 million	Annual combined U.S. federal and state spending to encourage apprenticeships
$200 billion	Annual combined U.S. federal and state spending on nonapprenticeship forms of post-secondary education

Source: Economist Robert Lerman. Used with permission.

Aim High, No Ceiling

Kevin Burton was one of the people I bumped into at the IBEW training center. Anyone who thinks that apprenticeship training tracks people into careers with limited upward mobility should meet this young woman (yes, Kevin is a she), who credits the training with changing her life for the better.

I first met Kevin in 2012 in Washington, D.C., at a U.S. Department of Labor event. At the time she was an instructor at the Lanham center. Kevin is one of those bright and ambitious individuals who wanted to go to college but who, as an eighteen-year-old, just couldn't get it all together. She had good grades and several honors courses under her belt but, like many recent high school graduates, didn't have a clear plan for the future. "I didn't know what I should study or how I would pay for college," she said. So after graduation she joined the U.S. Army National Guard, which trained her to repair radar equipment. After a year or so of active duty, she returned to the D.C. area and began looking for a job, keeping up her Guard obligations on weekends.

Kevin soon found a position at a private security company, but while the work paid well, it provided little challenge and no career development. "I would have been doing the same thing year after year," she said. After six months on the job she spotted a newspaper ad for an electrical apprenticeship program. That ad put her life onto a much different course.

Kevin applied to Local 26's apprentice program, but was not initially accepted. She decided to take advantage of the union's trainee program while she waited for the next cycle of apprentices to be selected. Kevin is living proof of the wisdom of the saying "If you at first don't succeed, try, try again."

The next round she was accepted and, as she hoped, a slot opened up. Kevin joined the five-year program. "The pay was good," she remembers. And it got better every year. In the first four years she learned everything from the theory of circuitry to practical application. She spent some days in the training center and other days learning on the job. Then, during her final year, as is customary with fifth-year apprentices, she worked exclusively for a single contractor, where she earned 80 percent of a journeyman electrician's hourly rate as she continued to learn and gain experience in the trade.

Upon finishing the program, Kevin, now a newly minted journeywoman, had more than enough work to keep her busy, and she was earning more money than she had ever anticipated. A qualified journeyman can elect to stay with their training employer, seek new opportunities, or start their own enterprise. But Kevin had a higher goal: She wanted to share what she had learned with others. Having had no mentors in her own family, she had been helped along by others over the years: high school teachers, apprentice instructors, and contractors. She wanted to help other young people in the same way. As she explained, "I wanted to extend a hand and help others, just as others had helped me." And so she began moonlighting at the Lanham training center, teaching some of the basics of electricity to pre-apprentice trainees and to early-stage apprentices. Kevin proved to be as good a teacher as she was an electrician and was soon offered a full-time position. Yet teaching young people only fueled her desire to further her own education, and in 2007, Kevin began undergraduate studies at the University of Maryland, earning a bachelor's degree in humanities four years later. In 2012, degree in hand, she was named as one of the center's assistant directors.

Kevin's story is an inspiring example of how apprenticeships aren't necessarily just for those who want to learn a trade, but also for those aspiring to professional, upwardly mobile careers. After all, here's a young person who had no family connections, advantages, or career counseling. But thanks to an inner spark, mentoring, determination, and structured training, she climbed into the middle class through a respected profession. And the story isn't yet complete. Eager to climb still more rungs on life's ladder, Kevin applied to several law schools and, in early 2013, was accepted by three, including George Washington University Law School, which she opted to attend. I expect that the next time I hear from Kevin, she'll be a successful attorney negotiating labor contracts or advocating ERISA (retirement) issues on behalf of her fellow electricians and their union. Her apprenticeship opened the door to all these opportunities, and Kevin walked on through.

Here's the take-away from Kevin's story: an apprenticeship creates no ceiling on continued achievement. If anything, it cultivates the maturity and confidence that young people need to aim higher and higher. And in this, Kevin's story is not unique; I know countless men and women who began their working lives as apprentices, practiced a trade, and then went on to higher education and/or to higher-level positions as managers or business owners. I can tell you that the working lives of the apprentice-trained people I know are every bit as fulfilling and well rewarded as those who followed the high-school-to-college track.

THE TEN-YEAR APPRENTICESHIP

One thing you quickly learn about Japan is that on-the-job training through an apprenticeship is taken very seriously. One of the most famous sushi restaurants in the world is Sukiyabashi Jiro in downtown Tokyo. There, the apprentice master (what we in the United States would think of as the head chef) Jiro Ono expects no less than a ten-year commitment from his apprentices. The restaurant has received an incredible three Michelin stars for six consecutive years. According to Michelin, the third star means it's worth visiting the country *just* to experience that restaurant. The fascinating documentary *Jiro Dreams of Sushi* follows the eighty-five-year-old sushi master Jiro in his relentless pursuit of perfection as he passes on his knowledge and skills to his star apprentice: his fifty-year-old son Yoshikazu.

The Economics of Apprenticeships

At this point you may be wondering whether apprentice wages are enough to live off during the years it takes to learn a trade. Well, in a nutshell, the apprentice pays no tuition and borrows no money, but receives a growing stream of earnings over a four-year training period. Upon completion of the program, he or she earns a respectable income, generally with progressive increases over a working lifetime. One study has shown that graduates of apprenticeship programs earn substantially more than other forms of skill training, including community college associate degree programs. By the calculation of that study, the person who completes an apprenticeship earns, in present-value terms, some $250,000 more in lifetime earnings than their nonapprenticed peers with only high school diplomas, when you take into account the earnings missed during the training period.

Compare this with the economics of a more traditional school-to-career path. As a student at a state-supported residential school, you'll be paying out $10,000 to $15,000 every year for four years (double that or more for a private college)—say, half of those outlays are yours and half is borrowed money. If you're lucky, you'll earn $3,000 each year in part-time or summer work, enough for books or perhaps a beverage fund. If you're a good student you'll end up four years later with a degree and around $30,000-plus in student loan debts (the national average). But this is only the beginning. It will now be time to write your résumé and start looking for a job, which could take months or even years.

On the other hand, let's say that you enroll in an apprenticeship. If you follow that path successfully, you'll pay nothing and earn somewhere around $25,000 a year. Four years later you will have a job, a nationally recognized certification of competence in your field, and, in all likelihood, an associate degree from a community college. You will have earned some $100,000 in wages over that time, and have no debts to pay. And since you already have a job, you won't have the chore of hunting for one (all the while living off your rapidly dwindling savings).

And how much do newly minted apprentices earn? Though every program is different, apprenticeships registered with a state or with the U.S. Department of Labor must provide a progressively increasing wage beginning at or above the minimum wage in the particular jurisdiction. As an example, here's the wage schedule of participants in the IBEW's five-year program in Massachusetts, where each year's wage is a percentage of a prevailing journeyman electrician's wage.

Percentage Earned of Full Journeyman's Wage

Year 1	40%
Year 2	50%
Year 3	55%
Year 4	65%
Year 5	70%

What does this mean in real numbers? The typical journeyman electrician wage in Massachusetts in 2013 was $50,000 to $55,000, depending on locality (plus an opportunity for overtime pay). Thus, at the low end, the annual apprentice wage for years one through five would be about $20,000, $25,000, $27,500, $32,500, and $35,000, respectively. An apprentice also receives wage increases when skills are mastered and on-the-job milestones are met. Although the table is based on five-year apprenticeships, many are four years, or even three. Some are now based on an apprentice's competence, rather than time.

Apprenticeships of the Future

Today's apprenticeship programs are becoming more sophisticated and progressive as highly specialized technical skills are becoming more and more valuable to employers. In fact, most of today's apprenticeships look nothing like the vision you might have in your head of two craftsmen wielding hammers huddled over a wooden workbench. The "one skill, one job" apprenticeships of old are being replaced by modern apprenticeships—those that impart deep technical and process knowledge. To see what a modern-day apprenticeship really looks like, we have to look no further than the sprawling $1.1 billion state-of-the-art auto plant Volkswagen built between 2009 and 2011 just outside Chattanooga, Tennessee, specifically designed for assembling the company's popular Passat sedan for the American market. The Volkswagen plant is now one of the area's largest employers with roughly three thousand full- and part-time personnel working there each day. But what's significant about these workers for our purposes is the fact that a small but growing number of them are apprentices in training; and although their numbers are still small at time of this writing, VW is counting on them to play a large part in the future success of its plant.

This innovative three-year training program is a collaboration between Volkswagen and nearby Chattanooga State Technical Community College. All of the training takes place on-site at the Volkswagen training academy with a twelve-to-one student-teacher ratio: lower than any public high school ratio and most college classrooms. After completing nine semesters, the final four of which consist of on-the-job training, for which they are paid, graduates receive a certificate recognized by the Association of German Chambers of Commerce and Industry, a job offer from Volkswagen, and an associate's degree in applied science and engineering technology from Chattanooga State.

I visited the Volkswagen Chattanooga Assembly Plant just a few months before the first class of their apprentices were scheduled to graduate, to see the quality and scope of Volkswagen's German-based program that had been transmitted onto the North American side of the Atlantic.

Upon arrival at the VW plant, I was greeted by staff members of the Volkswagen Academy Automation Mechatronics Program, who gave me a comprehensive tour of the assembly areas and the teaching facility. If you are picturing this backdrop right now, please let go of any image you might be having of a tour of greasy, dark, noisy rooms filled with underpaid workers on their feet toiling on production lines for exhausting twelve-hour shifts. Quite the opposite: The buildings are welcoming, spotless, ultramodern, well-lit, and built to Leadership in Energy and Environmental Design (LEED) Platinum standards. Twelve percent of the facility's energy requirements are supplied by an on-site photovoltaic array, and its recycling efforts include using the rainwater that hits the roof to flush toilets and cool equipment throughout the plant. The corridor linking the main entrance and the production area is lined with flat-screen monitors that remind everyone of how well the plant is doing relative to its performance metrics: finished vehicles versus plan, on-time vehicle completions, quality scores, the number of Passats shipped that day, and so forth. The production lines themselves are marvels of industrial engineering, along which energetic people and tireless robots and other machines work together to meet high standards of precision, safety, and efficiency. And it seems that wherever you look, the plant's motto, "Passion for detail," is boldly posted. Even Volkswagen's cafeteria is first-class—the best I've experienced in an industrial setting. In short, there is no question that VW-Chattanooga was designed to ensure surroundings conducive to producing world-class vehicles.

Although the tour of the plant was eye opening (and the chef in me could have spent hours looking over the state-of-the-art kitchens and facilities), I was eager to get to the Volkswagen Academy, the sparkling $40 million facility where the skills training takes place. The academy itself is housed within a 162,000-square-foot complex of classrooms and laboratory-like instruction areas, all within steps of the assembly plant. Every tool, vehicle component, conveyor, and system (robots, painting room, and so forth) that apprentices will ever encounter on the job can be found there. And just as in the plant itself, every tool and workbench is spotless and orderly from floor to ceiling; you won't find a screwdriver, a paper cup, or a length of used wiring lying about anywhere. As one instructor told me, "Here we have a place for everything, and everything is in its place."

The first phase of apprentice training at the academy speaks volumes about the academy's rigor and the company's workplace values it fosters. Right at the start of the first fifteen-week machining semester, trainees are assigned a labor-intensive hands-on project that aims to develop patience and inculcate each student with the virtues of discipline, precision, and uncompromising attention to detail, such as fashioning a small hand vise out of pieces of steel using nothing but a blueprint, handsaws, files, and measuring tools—no easy task. As one trainer said to me: "Some eighteen- to twenty-four-year-olds lack the discipline for this type of work." Volkswagen designs the program specifically to help those students develop it.

VW's program is methodical and progressive. Each apprentice receives training in a core curriculum of safety, quality control, problem solving, electricity, metalworking, machining, and so forth. They're even given fitness training to increase flexibility, endurance, and physical strength. From that point, instruction and hands-on work diverge along two separate trajectories. One focuses on building the body of the automobile itself: constructing mechanical and electrical systems, engine diagnostics, hydraulics, welding, bodywork, and many other skills. Most of the apprentices who follow this "car mechatronics" track will become multidisciplined troubleshooters in the automotive assembly plant. Another, larger group is immersed in all the skills required to keep the automated plant and its infrastructure running smoothly: what is known as "automation mechatronics." This second group concentrates on electronics, programmable logic controls, pneumatics, robotics, computer-controlled machining, fault analysis, and more.

Apprentices are given regular performance reviews and mentoring over the course of the three-year program, and complete their learning with a major team-based project. The academy also trains VW dealer personnel to service the latest technology being built into the company's vehicles. Once trained, these individuals go back to their dealerships and pass on their learning to their associates.

This skill-building blueprint was adapted from the dual system of classroom and workplace learning that Volkswagen and other European companies have finetuned over many decades. As one trainer put it, "We picked the best parts of both traditional German and

American apprenticeships." To that end, two apprentice trainers from Volkswagen German operations came over in 2010 to work with Chattanooga State to create the program.

Of the program's nine semesters, five take place in the academy and four in the plant itself. Apprentices must be at least college age and have graduated high school in order to apply.[4] But the program is in no way limited to eighteen-year-old high school graduates. As Ilker Subasi, one of the current trainers at the academy, told me, VW Chattanooga apprentices currently range in age from eighteen to forty-eight, with most being twenty-four or twenty-five; the program has no age ceiling for applicants.

Unlike its counterparts in European countries (where apprenticeships are more common and enjoy higher standing), the U.S. academy must conduct ongoing outreach activities in order to attract and bring on board qualified candidates. Even at a time when the Chattanooga area's economy is suffering from 8 percent overall unemployment (even higher among young people), the program suffers from the same dearth of applicants as many of the other skills-based pathways in our "college for everyone" society. As Ralph Gwaltney, coordinator of the academy's two mechatronics programs and a faculty member at Chattanooga State, described it to me, while the company routinely welcomes busloads of high school students who enjoy visiting the academy and taking tours of the plant, "We know that the decision makers are often the parents or grandparents." So they "periodically host evening open houses so that the young people who are interested can give their family members a chance to see the place and learn about our program."

Six months after my visit, I learned of two exciting additions to the apprenticeship program in Chattanooga. Graduates are no longer limited to jobs at Chattanooga; they are now eligible to request assignments to VW facilities in other parts of the world. Two members of the first graduating class had, in fact, put in for an assignment to an international plant—the type of career opportunity that college grads wait years for and that, prior to Volkswagen, was almost unheard of at blue-collar or technician levels. The second is a recent program that allows apprentice graduates to work toward a bachelor's degree in engineering and business administration.

This program is still in its early days, so time will tell how well it all plays out. But because Volkswagen has been educating apprentices for so long, my bet is that the company will get what it wants and more from its investment in the Chattanooga academy—and so will its increasing numbers of highly skilled graduates.

Why "Mentored" Apprenticeships?

For almost a decade I have had a front-row seat to the design and development of cutting-edge apprenticeship opportunities that offer people the chance to find their passion and parlay that passion into fulfilling and well-paying careers. Over the years, I've found that while virtually all those who complete an apprenticeship program find themselves in demand and employable upon completion, sadly, there are some who never complete their training. It is an issue that has challenged and frustrated me over the past few years: Why is it that people drop out of skills programs, specifically apprenticeships?

There is no question there are obvious indicators warning that a person is at risk of dropping out of an apprenticeship program: high absenteeism, falling behind in studies, or even just a change of mind or loss of interest in the job. But I've found that the key factor in predicting whether a person will complete or drop out of an apprenticeship program is not level of motivation or even performance; it's the presence or lack of mentorship.

When I talk about mentorship, I'm not just talking about the kind of boss-employee relationship that is a given in any work situation. An apprenticeship role offers a unique opportunity to develop a special breed of learning relationship: one formed for the sole purpose of providing support, expertise, and practical experience. I've found that those who get the most out of apprenticeship programs are those who enjoy the guidance of a person with whom there is no reporting or supervisory relationship, but who can act as a sounding board to talk to about development opportunities, and help the mentee adjust to situations and work though everyday challenges.

This is why, in Australia for instance, many apprenticeship programs are operated by group training organizations that match apprentices with skilled mentors across a broad selection of occupations. The Institute for Workplace Skills and Innovation operates a GTO called WPC Group (Work Place Connect), and through it we are able to ensure our apprentices are paired with experienced mentors like Greg Payne and others who draw on their own deep industry experience to counsel protégés and keep them on track. Greg was a qualified culinary tradesman who then branched into teaching at a local technical college before taking on the mentoring role. Greg and many like him help bridge the gap between new employee and employer expectations by actually visiting workplaces and talking to both the apprentices and supervisors about their progress and any barriers that could be interfering with their immediate and long-term success.

WHAT'S A GTO?

In Australia, group training organizations are usually community-based, not-for-profit organizations that directly employ apprentices and then place them with host employers. The GTO takes care of the apprentice's wages, entitlements, and insurance and provides field-based mentoring. The GTOs also manage recruitment and training enrollment and even take the apprentices back if things don't work out. Particularly small and medium-size businesses find this arrangement attractive as it saves them time on administration and lowers their risk of turnover. The Host Employer pays one weekly invoice that includes the apprentice's wage and a small management fee (around 10 percent): a model that works financially as the GTOs pool the management fee and the employer government incentives (similar to the South Carolina tax incentive, in this case a $1,500 commencement payment and $2,500 completion payment for each apprentice). GTOs also assist governments in engaging and employing people from underrepresented groups within the community and act as a safety net for apprentices should they not be able to complete an apprenticeship with an employer. This model has been successfully adapted internationally to suit local labor market conditions.

Mentors also play the role of advocate and, on occasion, mediator. They look for—and are skilled at spotting—the signs of doubt, fear, and frustration that apprentices, like many new employees (and their supervisors), might have over the course of a placement. This way, they can intervene in a productive and helpful way before problems grow, conflicts occur, and things begin to feel hopeless.

Let me share a powerful story that demonstrates just how much of a difference a mentor can make in the life of a young apprentice. I know of one young man who walked away from his automotive apprenticeship just weeks after commencement. The official cancellation paperwork under employer comment read "poor attitude, not suitable." This seemed unlikely to me, so I asked one of the program mentors, Paul Brook, to delve deeper. He found out the employer was frustrated that the apprentice (who requested not to be named here) had "made mistake after mistake" when measuring liquids and coolants. Turned out what was really going on was that the young man had literacy and numeracy problems and was unable to read basic measurements. He had learned how to cover up the problem enough to get the job, but not keep it. He knew he needed help, but he didn't know how to ask. So rather than face embarrassment, he chose to walk away. But with Paul's guidance, he developed a plan for overcoming this barrier and resumed an apprenticeship a month later. Today, he is one of his new company's best performing employees.

A final word on mentors: They are not just for newly minted apprentices; I am proud to say that I still have a mentor. I strongly recommend you give it a try.

Apprentice Program at Starbucks

While most apprenticeships are three or four years in duration and involve both on-the-job and classroom-based instruction, every so often a company will design a shorter program to meet its particular needs. While the graduates of these abbreviated programs may not come away with full mastery of a trade, the programs present an opportunity to earn money while embarking on a clear, defined career path—and learn a variety of new and transferable skills along the way.

Starbucks in the United Kingdom, for example, has designed a program that does much more than train people in the art of roasting beans; its graduates complete a crash course in the practical business skills that position them to manage or even start their own businesses someday. The initial program is twelve months long and offers apprenticeship qualifications in both barista mastery and customer service, and there is also the option for the apprentice to stay on longer to complete additional certifications in subjects like web design, accounting, marketing, sales, and management. As with other successful programs, there is on-the-job as well as off-site learning and mentoring, and a strong focus on the so-called soft skills required to succeed in today's workplace (punctuality, working with others, and so forth). Starbucks apprentices learn the nuts and bolts of running both the technical and customer service sides of a small retail business, including communication and team skills, problem solving, conflict resolution, and the workplace etiquette that so many young people need to develop.

That know-how puts Starbucks graduates on a company career trajectory that could advance them into higher levels of Starbucks management as shift managers, store managers, district managers, account executives, marketers, and so forth. And, as you'd imagine, the skills they learn are highly transferable to other retail and customer service businesses. So, in a very real way, a Starbucks apprenticeship is like a small business management program you'd find at your local community college, but with a regular paycheck, paid vacations, health care benefits, and no tuition costs.

New apprentices earn the same salary as entry-level baristas while they learn through on-the-job training, workbook assignments, webinars, some classroom instruction, and regular coaching. And the program offers its graduates great prospects for full-time employment by the company; in early 2013 Starbucks announced a commitment to hire one thousand apprentices by the end of 2014.

Once an apprentice is hired, they not only have a permanent job at Starbucks; they even qualify to receive stock options to purchase shares in the company (through the company's Bean Stock program) as well as retirement, vacation, and other employee benefits. The company's motivation is quite logical. It needs a strong "bench" of personnel capable of managing its expanding universe of coffee shops: people who possess not only operating skills but who have a proven ability to embrace the Starbucks culture. And they know that the best way to get both qualities—skills and cultural buy-in—is to build them internally.

Starbucks is just one example of a company that has opened its eyes to the fact that rather than scour the existing pool of workers for people with the right skills to do the jobs the company needs, a far more effective way to build a strong workforce is to "skill up" their existing workforce by offering on-the-job learning. In the next chapter you'll read about companies in other countries and sectors that have similarly recognized that reality, and are developing programs that represent a fourth educational pathway that holds incredible opportunity for those *already* in the workplace: state-of-the-art on-the-job skill building and training.

6

Skilling Up

Readers living in urban areas might be familiar with Whole Foods Market, a Texas-based grocery company specializing in natural and organic foods. Since its founding in 1980 at a single location, the enterprise has expanded to more than 370 stores employing nearly eighty thousand people in the United States, Canada, and the United Kingdom. As a former chef, I enjoy wandering through Whole Foods stores. Those visits are always a feast for the eye and an opportunity to encounter interesting new ingredients to spark my culinary imagination.

Whole Foods is as popular with employees as it is with foodies—so much so that it has made the *Fortune* magazine list of "100 Best Companies to Work For" *seventeen* years in a row. One reason, other than the good pay and generous benefits, might be that the company has quite a few unique and interesting—one could even say mouthwatering—jobs. For example, most of the company's twelve global regions have a position called a local forager, who is something like a matchmaker between local producers and growers and Whole Foods. There is also a global spice coordinator, who, among other duties, travels the world locating the best paprika, coriander, nutmeg, and other spices that make our meals so much more exciting. There is also a global cheese buyer, who has similar responsibilities in her own special corner of the food world. And, in the Pacific Northwest region, some stores have an employee, or "team member," as they are called, in charge of a mobile store that brings fresh fruits, vegetables, and other healthy products (as well as nutritional education) to customers and communities that might otherwise have no access to them. All of the jobs require skills not typically taught in classrooms.

I recently spoke with Joe Rogoff, president of Whole Foods' Pacific Northwest region, which includes Washington State, Oregon, and British Columbia, about how employees learn these highly specialized and unusual skills. By way of an answer, Rogoff told me about his own background. He got his start in the grocery trade back in the 1970s when he was a food co-op volunteer in rural Sonoma County, California. A college student at the time, he liked the grocery business so much that left his books and classrooms behind and began working full-time in the co-op. "I found my home," he told me, "and I discovered all my skills through work—organizing, displaying merchandise in appealing ways, and creating win-win relationships with suppliers, customers, and employees." Before long, Rogoff was managing seven natural food stores in the San Francisco Bay Area. When Whole Foods acquired those stores, he stayed on, assuming greater and greater responsibilities and learning more and more specialized skills over the years.

Joe Rogoff's education in the grocery business mirrors Whole Foods' approach to employee development. "We're a skills- and experience-based enterprise," he told me. New people learn by doing. While acknowledging the importance of academic learning, he emphasized that what a person learns through their hands-on experience in the store is what matters most. As an example, he recounted the case of a young friend who had gone to college, earned a master's degree, and then went to work for Whole Foods. Her education, however, didn't put her even a hair ahead of her peers because so much of what matters in retail grocery must be learned on the job. "Generations of grocers have learned the business through mentoring and informal apprenticeships, and we've done the same here," he said. "Classroom training has a place, but on-the-job experience and eagerness to learn new things is what gets Whole Foods' people to where they need to be."

Whole Foods put a high value on diversity of learning experiences. "That's how people find their path—their purpose," said Rogoff. "They find it by being exposed to lots of things, which is why so many people come to Whole Foods for a job but end up finding a career."

The Whole Foods story is just one more example of how people can earn, learn, and grow in an interesting, dynamic workplace environment without the benefit of a four-year college degree. Few of the company's positions require one, and many of its leaders and executives—people like Joe Rogoff—are quite successful without them. At Whole Foods, acquiring skills, a passion for one's work, a sense of purpose, and an eagerness to learn and excel matter far more. And that's true just about everywhere, as you'll learn from the stories of companies and individuals you'll read in this chapter.

Operation Strawberries

When we think about vocational and technical education, we normally picture high school shop classes filled with high school students. But, in reality, skills-based education is not merely for the young adult; it's for anyone, at any age or stage in their career, who wants to shore up their skill set to remain employable and competitive in today's rapidly changing job market and volatile economic landscape.

Due in part to the rapid technological change and automation that are the hallmark of our modern era, many skills once prized and valued in the workplace are rapidly becoming obsolete—even analytical skills that require advanced education. Software programs packed with artificial intelligence and complex algorithms are now able to handle the work that highly educated and well-paid knowledge workers once did. For example, decisions on many types of bank loan applications that used to involve trained credit analysts working over several hours can now be made in a heartbeat and at a fraction of the cost with specialized software. Similarly, many tax preparers in the United States have watched with dismay as TurboTax and similar software programs have decreased their client bases. Today's technology enables these programs to incorporate all the arcane rules of the tax code—knowledge that tax preparers spend years learning and mastering—and reduce them to a series of binary digits that allows any individual to input their income, deductions, tax estimates paid, and so forth, as prompted, and bingo, their tax forms are ready for filing. Similar software is finding its way into the business of insurance underwriting, recruitment and human resources, journalism, and even medical diagnosis. In general, any job that involves a repetitive series of steps or a complex set of rules is in danger of being automated by machinery or software. The result being that even experienced, long-employed individuals in a variety of fields are waking up to find their jobs suddenly in danger of disappearing. Of course, no one individual can single-handedly halt technological progress or stem the tide of automation. But what you *can* do, if you're one of the tens of thousands of workers facing this situation, is invest in yourself and your future by making yourself so indispensable to your current or future employer that no computer could ever possibly replace you. How? By taking the initiative to arm yourself with the most cutting-edge, most relevant, and least automatable skills.

But "skilling up" isn't the silver bullet only for those

confronting the threat of automation or outsourcing; it's a smart career move for any worker or professional who has outgrown their current position and is seeking something more. What new skills must you master to conquer the next leg of your career journey? Think of the electrician working at a medium-size firm. At first he's content doing the job he was trained to do: wiring homes or offices, troubleshooting, making repairs, and so forth. But as his proficiencies grow, so do his responsibilities. Eventually his skills as an electrician are less important than his ability to manage other people, handle the finances of the growing enterprise, and deal with customers. Suddenly, this skilled electrician finds himself in need of a new skill set if he wants to advance to the next level in his burgeoning career.

One common theme throughout this book is that successful careers are built on the desire and discipline to learn at any age and at every stage of one's life. I believe that when we find the career path we are meant to follow, luck turns to opportunity and the adage of "It's just a job" changes to "I'm passionate about my career." This passion is what motivates us to continuously learn new skills.

For me, the right career path began in the real world of cooking and culinary arts, not four years in a classroom. But my years as an apprentice chef were just the beginning of my on-the-job education. In my final year of apprenticeship, I was given the responsibility of supervising a new group of apprentices. I knew right away I needed more education to acquire the supervisory skills required to be successful in that role. So I enrolled in the hotel's in-house "train the trainer" program, which the hotel had implemented to help existing employees refresh, reboot, and upgrade their skill sets to stay relevant and ready to meet the challenges and opportunities that the ever-evolving hospitality industry presented.

My earliest on-the-job training experience was something called "Operation Strawberries." This was an exercise in which the hotel's entire operational staff—everyone from the chefs to the housekeepers to the receptionists—was invited to spend a complimentary night in the hotel as a guest, dine in the restaurant, and experience everything from a guest's perspective. As an apprentice, this was pretty exciting. There I was, in a junior suite with breathtaking views of the city skyline, eating my oversized bowl of room service strawberries (an old tradition from which the operation got its name), reveling in the excellent career choice I had made. But Operation Strawberries was much more than just a chance to experience a night in the lap of luxury. It taught me how each role in the hotel worked, and how *my* job contributed to the overall guest experience. In the process, I connected with other employees who I may not have otherwise met. In doing so—though I didn't realize it at the time—I started building my first professional network, one that still serves me well all these years later. For example, it was on Operation Strawberries that I first met Lucas Glanville, a young aspiring chef who later returned to London to work at the Michelin-starred restaurant Le

Gavroche, started by Albert and Michel Roux. Lucas is now the executive chef at the luxurious Grand Hyatt hotel in Singapore. Recently, I had the need to reach out to my network to find an employer willing to host a young aspiring apprentice who had been awarded an international scholarship. One email to Lucas and the job was done.

Operation Strawberries was just one of many on-the-job training experiences I've undertaken at various points along my career. Because no matter how much I learned or how many skills I acquired in any given workplace, each time I moved into a new job, got promoted into a new position, or transitioned into an adjacent industry, I would inevitably find that I needed additional skills in order to be successful. The truth is, no matter what career path you're on or what industry you're in, and whether you switch jobs once every two decades or once every year, in a world where industries are rapidly transformed and upended and technology is advancing as fast as it is, *staying employable, valuable, and competitive requires the constant acquisition of new skills.* I'll never forget what Anton Mosimann, the onetime *maître chef de cuisines* at London's Dorchester Hotel on Park Lane, once said to me: "Nicholas, don't wait for your ship to come in— swim out to it." From that day on, I took advantage of every learning opportunity any subsequent employer offered, and I couldn't be more happy that I did.

Fortunately, today many leading companies in the United States and around the world are offering their existing workforce the opportunity to "skill up"—to upgrade their skill sets to meet the changing demands of the workplace—in much the same way. These on-the-job training programs are typically a blend of the innovative educational and hands-on learning methods mentioned throughout his book. Of course, companies aren't merely offering these programs out of the goodness of their hearts. While employees leave these programs with education as well as opportunities, companies get a well-trained, highly skilled workforce poised to compete in our global economy. Smart companies know that skilling up their existing workforce, rather than going back to the labor pool for people with advanced and updated skills, not only reduces the cost of turnover but allows them to ensure that their workers are being educated in *the precise skills the company needs*.

The companies in the following pages are examples of what I see as the gold standard of on-the-job skills-based training. Think of them as a brochure of options to consider if you think it's time to reboot your skill set, whether you want to advance to a better position in your chosen field, secure your position if it's threatened by automation or outsourcing, or are a mature worker looking to launch your career in an exciting new positive direction. These companies provide tangible examples of the types of opportunities—from community-based courses to hands-on internships or externships to 24/7 online learning—that employers are putting into place to skill up their employees.

Whether you live in the United States, Europe, Asia,

Canada, the United Kingdom, or Australia, such opportunities can be found in your own backyard if you do your homework. With this book as your guide, all you need is a genuine interest in your own personal and career development, a willingness to reach out to those in the know, and the motivation to put in the time, energy, and effort to become your best at what you do. As a human resources professional, I know that doors open up to people who are serious about adding value to an organization—and at the same time invest in their own potential.

American Infrastructure, STIHL, Siemens, MGM Resorts International, and others have excellent programs already in place and demonstrate the new and exciting opportunities emerging for ambitious professionals wishing to upgrade their skill sets, boost their earning power, and accelerate their careers.

Solid Foundations for Successful Careers

American Infrastructure, a privately owned Pennsylvania-based heavy construction business, is a civil construction company and material supplier serving the U.S. mid-Atlantic region. In other words, it builds roads, bridges, water treatment plants, pipelines, and other big stuff!

Middle-skilled workers in the United States have a long history of building the big stuff. It was skilled workers who laid the tracks on the railways that crisscrossed the nation after the Civil War. It was skilled workers who dug the Panama Canal, one of the largest and most complex engineering projects ever undertaken. During the Great Depression, it was millions of skilled workers who added to the nation's backbone of highways, bridges, airports, dams, and the electrification system through the federal Public Works Administration. During that same period, two million more transformed the landscape and national parks through work in the Civilian Conservation Corps. And after World War II it was a brand-new generation of skilled workers who constructed the U.S. Interstate Highway System, the most ambitious infrastructure plan in human history to that time. All through real-world on-the-job training.

It's heartening to know that there are still companies around that are committed to training their workers in the skills it takes to build big stuff. American Infrastructure is one of them.

AI came to my attention because of its reputation for its commitment to developing the competencies of its roughly 1,800 employees. *Training* magazine consistently ranks it among its "Top 125" companies for employee development, a ranking that takes into account both quantitative and qualitative measures such as tuition assistance, training infrastructure, the number of trainers, employee turnover and retention, training budget relative to payroll spending, and how closely training is aligned with business objectives, to name just a few metrics. In 2013, AI was rated number one in the human resources component of the award and had the ninth highest over-all score of the Top 125.

AI's success in employee development is the outcome of a deliberate strategy. That strategy, the inspiration of CEO A. Ross Myers, took shape in the early 2000s as part of a broader process-improvement initiative. Myers reasoned that the company's employees were at least as important as the processes they used for creating customer value; they, too, should strive toward continual improvement. And so today every employee has a personal career map pointing them toward progressively greater competence—and higher-value work. CEO Myers continues to champion the cause.

Each step along an employee's one-to-seven-year map is matched to specific training or educational experiences. Some of those learning experiences, such as "heavy equipment operations," are available in-house through regularly scheduled courses. Others, such as certificate programs and college course work, are provided online or in external settings. The company provides 100 percent reimbursement for any external education and training that aligns with the needs of the business. These activities are orchestrated by Jamie Leitch, director of career development and training, and housed within a virtual Continuous Learning Center. They even have curriculum charts tied to positions, Jamie told me. "So if an employee is looking at a different or higher-level position, he or she can go online and see what courses are required or recommended as preparation."

The result is that just about everyone in this enterprise is highly skilled, from the engineers down. But it's the tradespeople—concrete workers, pipe layers, heavy equipment operators, welders, electricians, truck drivers, and the like—who form the backbone of operations. "Finding them," said Jamie, "is a struggle, even in this economy. Everyone is competing for talent." To attract the skilled people it needs, AI works closely with vocational high schools, postsecondary technical schools, and community colleges who provide external training through the Continuous Learning Center.

All this attention to employee development is expensive, but the payoff for AI has eclipsed the costs. It enjoys a first-rate skilled workforce and an impressive level of employee retention. In today's workplace, what worker would ever want to leave a company that has invested so heavily in them and their future?

Hats off to American Infrastructure and employers like it.

Attract, Train, and Develop

By now you know I started my career in the hospitality and tourism industry as an apprentice chef. But like most of us starting out, I didn't realize at the time that I had chosen to start my career journey in one of the most exciting, diverse, and dynamic industries there is. This is true now more than ever, as these thriving industries offer young adults, midlife career changers—anyone passionate about food and travel, for that matter—a wide variety of opportunities for launching and building long-term careers. Today, thanks to the explosion of a global food and wine culture and a resurgence of interest in travel, many tourism and hospitality employers are investing heavily in attracting, training, and developing the best people they can. Astute employers know that a skilled workforce is the key to a true competitive advantage—particularly in a business where the quality of your customer service can make the difference between success and failure. During the last economic downturn, for instance, I know of one five-star hotel that stopped investing in entry-level skills. They stopped all frontline training and let many of their entry-level workers go, gambling that they could simply replace them when the economy turned around. What they failed to foresee was that when demand picked up, they'd be caught short and forced to pay top dollar to buy some of those skills back.

Hospitality and tourism is a broad and growing industry and a huge source of employment in many countries. In Australia, for instance, one in fourteen people of working age are directly employed in the tourism, hospitality, or related industries, and many European countries battered by the recent economic meltdown—such as Greece, for example—are looking to tourism to lead them to economic recovery.

People who choose careers in the hospitality industry have many roles to select from—both what is called front of house (what the guest often can see) and back of house (the operations behind the scenes). Both require skills that can be learned and honed only through real-world experience and on-the-job training.

Let me take you behind the scenes of a leading hospitality employer and show you what a skilled career in this profession is all about. MGM Resorts International is one of the world's largest resort-casino, gaming, and entertainment companies in the world, with fifteen resorts located in Las Vegas alone and other operations throughout the United States, as well as a new enterprise in the Chinese city of Macau. In Las Vegas, their iconic properties include the Bellagio, Aria, Mandalay Bay, and the MGM Grand. They receive tens of thousands of guests a year and are known for the consistency of their customer service. I wanted to see what was driving the excellent customer service experience firsthand. Not surprisingly, I discovered a company that considers skills training and development a business imperative. The company not only understands the value of hiring, promoting, retaining, and developing its employees; it has taken skills training to another level with their creation of MGM Resorts University, through which it provides comprehensive skills training and ongoing professional development for more than sixty-six thousand employees. With a team of around thirty full-time training professionals, MGM offers skills-development opportunities on all levels and in areas ranging from food and beverage services and hotel and casino operations to retail, HR, and finance. Courses include soft skills, computer training, life skills development, workplace English, GED prep, and leadership and career advancement programs. They even offer an online bachelor's degree in strengths-based management.

Through their industry-first intensive diversity training program, MGM fosters an environment of inclusion, teamwork, and mutual respect that encourages each employee and student to reach their potential and achieve long-term career goals. And while the classes aren't free, MGM offers full-time employees more than $2,000 a year in tuition reimbursement.

In addition to skills training and professional development for employees, MGM University offers paid internships for current college students and graduates. These internships emphasize active skills and career development through hands-on work, as well as exceptional networking and travel opportunities. For example, many of the interns work with *Fortune* 500 executives, through the challenging Executive Associate Program. And in the Hospitality Internship Program and Management Associate Program, interns are not only assigned advisers and mentors for the full length of the program but are transitioned directly into entry-level positions with MGM as assistant managers or equivalent leadership roles.

This comprehensive approach to skills training and professional development is creating real pathways to management and leadership positions at MGM—while at the same time helping MGM maintain its stellar reputation of customer service and seamless guest experience.

From Building Tools to Building a Rewarding Career

If you have ever had to do maintenance around the home, I'm willing to bet you have at least one STIHL-brand product sitting in your garage or shed. Well-known for being a leading producer of high-quality chain saws, STIHL has a well-earned reputation. I have always admired the company for the quality and reliability of their products, and I personally own several of them.

Having grown from less than fifty employees in the mid-1970s, STIHL Inc. (STIHL), the headquarters for the U.S. operations for the worldwide STIHL Group, today employs more than 2,100 people nationwide. Thanks to its proximity to Virginia's many military bases and shipyards, the company has access to a large and highly skilled labor pool. Even so, finding people with the right training to participate in its high-speed and highly specialized manufacturing operations hasn't been easy.

Which is why STIHL has decided to implement a wide-ranging employee training and development program, one that offers more than one hundred in-house technical and nontechnical courses (such as supervision, time management, and leadership) yearly in a regular cycle. The training is carefully aligned to frontline manufacturing operations needs, ensuring that the programs deliver the precise skills to reliably improve workplace performance. In other words, rather than roll the dice that workers from the outside labor pool will meet specific job requirements, STIHL has decided to skill up from the inside. Or as Debbie Kremers, director of human resources for STIHL Inc., put it, "We've relied on our own training to supply the STIHL skilled workforce."

Like American Infrastructure, STIHL's strong focus on learning and development is driven by bottom-line imperatives, such as increased productivity and a commitment to company-wide safety. Its training programs are extensive and range from hands-on technical specialties—such as mechatronics and robotics—to more process-specific practices such as injection molding of plastics and computer technology, including SAP and other business software. The courses are all delivered in a collaborative environment and framed around real-world scenarios and practical applications; the goal is for every employee who undergoes a training program to walk out of that room ready to put those skills immediately into practice.

The instruction takes place on different levels and at different locations throughout the organization, including at the company's manufacturing facility in Virginia Beach, Virginia, and in training centers across the United States. And the courses aren't just open to supervisors or managers, as training programs tend to be at some companies; every employee in the company—no matter their rank or position—has equal access to most training and development opportunities. Training is an ongoing process of improvement, and the company's frontline improvement program Idea Plus, for example, is popular with workers on the production line, who enjoy the opportunity to learn skills that will help them improve their own personal productivity, as well as come up with creative ways to improve the efficiency of the entire line. Originators of successful ideas are rewarded by up to 25 percent of the savings achieved. The company has even extended its training programs beyond just workers within the company to developing specific training programs for its retailers as well, including the STIHL MasterWrench Service® certification program for retailer service technicians.

One thing you quickly learn at STIHL is that there is no training simply for training's sake. Every single program or initiative is carefully and deliberately aimed at equipping STIHL's workforce with the skills that will be critical to their—and the company's—success.

And this staunch commitment to developing a skilled workforce comes straight from the top. Fred Whyte, president of STIHL Inc., is a strong advocate of skilled careers. "In North America, we have a certain 'sheepskin psychosis' and tend to ascribe too much value to purely academic credentials. Consequently, it can be difficult for educational institutions specializing in skilled trades to attract students. This seems quite extraordinary given the appreciation we feel when our plumbing is professionally repaired, the wiring in our homes expertly installed, and our cars and small engines properly serviced. The value of skilled technicians is obvious and essential," comments Whyte.

Beyond their varied and diverse on-site courses, the company also offers online distance learning through Tooling U for direct employees and through the aptly named STIHL iCademy® for its retailers. The award-winning iCademy offers eighty interactive classes—many of which include video and multimedia—designed specifically for retailers and their employees but available to distributors and internal employees as well. Since the site's launch, thirty-eight thousand registered users have taken over a million online quizzes or exams. The cost to the retailer? Zero dollars. That's the beauty of an online course—once it's been created, it costs virtually nothing to replicate or disseminate to almost infinite users in just about any location. No wonder John Keeler, the company's national training manager, saw it as the perfect solution to ensuring all frontline representatives have access to updated, relevant training (we will come back to the virtues of online learning later in this chapter).

STIHL isn't just looking out for its current workplace needs; this forward-looking company is already thinking about how to ensure a supply of the skilled labor they might need ten, twenty, or even forty years into the future. For example, STIHL's Virginia Beach facility is an active partner in a career and technical education partnership with local community educators. In addition to sending instructors to teach at the nearby community college, the company holds Manufacturing Technology Summer Camps to build interest and engage students—

that is, future employees—as young as twelve or thirteen years old in the opportunities that exist in the modern manufacturing industry.

New Skills at Work Initiative

In December 2013, leading financial services firm JPMorgan Chase & Co. launched New Skills at Work, a global workforce training initiative aimed at addressing the skills gap from both supply and demand perspectives. The $250 million initiative is the largest of its kind to ever come from the private sector, highlighting the reality that skills training is the way forward for employers and those in the market for rewarding, well-paying careers across many high-growth industries.

New Skills at Work is a revolutionary approach to addressing the skills gap, combining research and data analysis with public and private partnerships to identify job opportunities in urban centers throughout the United States and Europe, including Chicago, Los Angeles, Miami, New York, San Francisco, and London. At the same time, it also invests in training programs that enable the local workforce to gain the skills needed to fill these roles.

The initiative is being led by Chauncy Lennon, senior program director for workforce development and managing director for global philanthropy at JPMorgan

Chase, and the advisory council is led by JPMC chairman and CEO Jamie Dimon and cochaired by Melody Barnes, former director of the White House Domestic Policy Council. The initiative's national partners include nonprofits that have already proven effective in training Americans for today's employment opportunities. Year Up is one such nonprofit, chosen for their job-training investments in youth ages sixteen to twenty-four, as well as underemployed adults or those seeking career advancement or transition.

"Addressing the skills gap can be one of our most powerful tools for reducing unemployment and creating more broadly shared prosperity," said Jamie Dimon. "JPMorgan is using its best assets, including industry intelligence and strong partnerships in local communities, to provide a platform for employers, educators, and workforce participants to help people gain the skills they need to succeed."

The initiative's Workforce Readiness Gap Reports bridge the distance between employer demand and effectively tailored skills training programs by identifying critical vacancies in local job markets and the skills needed to fill them. This data is then used to inform regional strategies on both the demand and supply sides of the labor market. Demand-side partners include local industry and sector associations, chambers of commerce, and National Fund for Workforce Solutions partnerships. On the supply side, partners range from community colleges and skilled training providers to local chapters of national training programs, such as the National Academies Foundation, Year Up, and YouthBuild, among others.

"At JPMorgan Chase, we spend our days working with businesses and in communities," Lennon explained. "We hear over and over about the challenges these companies are having trying to find the skilled workforce they need. So it became clear to us that we could contribute to solving an important challenge—while also helping to address unemployment and expand economic opportunity—by using our resources and reach to identify the sectors and occupations where the skills gap is the most acute, galvanize business engagement, and support education and training providers helping job seekers to gain in-demand skills. We know that helping workers gain the skills they need is only one part of the solution to the unemployment challenge, but it is an area we can do something about right now."

The landmark New Skills at Work initiative demonstrates the need for skilled specialists in a variety of interesting and exciting fields—from advanced manufacturing to health care to information technology—throughout the United States and Europe. For young people just choosing a career as well as adults transitioning into a new career, this initiative is filling the gap between opportunity and education—preparing the skilled workforce so vital to our future.

The Siemens Charlotte Energy Hub

Siemens is one of the world's largest and most diversified industrial companies, with operating units in everything from automation and building technologies to consumer products, health care technology, drive technologies, and financial services. It is also a leading provider of wind and hydropower equipment and highly efficient natural gas- and steam-powered electrical generating turbines. Those turbines, with capacities ranging from 150 to 1,600 megawatts, are marvels of engineering and precision machining. Many are built at the company's Charlotte, North Carolina, plant, and shipped to power utilities throughout the world.

I spent some time at the Charlotte plant not out of some personal fascination with these six-hundred-ton pieces of steel and wiring that are amazing works of human ingenuity but because of Siemens's reputation for leadership in skilling up its employees.

It all began in 2010, when Siemens committed to making a $300 million–plus investment in plant expansion. Not long after they signed on the dotted line, they realized they faced a serious human resources problem. "All Siemens operating divisions in the United States were facing the same problem," said Pamela Howze, the plant's manager of training and development at the time. "Baby boomer employees were approaching retirement, and there weren't enough technically trained young people in the area to replace them." By her calculation, 40 percent of the skilled workforce at the Siemens Charlotte Energy Hub was *already* eligible for retirement prior to the plant's expansion, and the majority of new blood graduating into the labor pool simply didn't have the skills or experience the plant needed.

"It's easy to get entry-level people, and we have lots of them, but difficult to recruit skilled workers," said Pamela. "So I started thinking about how we could take the people we already have in entry-level jobs and build up their skills and prepare them for higher-level jobs." The solution, she realized, was to develop a suite of training programs to fill its expanded human resources needs from *within the company.*

Siemens developed a raft of technical training and e-learning courses, and even set about developing an innovative apprenticeship program much like the ones described in the last chapter. The company also gave employees access to more formal leadership development training, such as a "train-the-trainer" program that offers managers and team leaders the opportunity to travel to Siemens's headquarters in Germany to learn how to operate new equipment. Employees then return to Charlotte to pass on their newly learned skills to the workforce back at the plant.

The training programs incorporate some of the latest cutting-edge e-learning tools available today, such as Tooling U-SME, a commercially available platform that offers a wide-ranging set of online courses that Siemens employees can take, either from ten workstations inside the plant or via their home computers or laptops at a time that suits them. Many of the workers I spoke to reported that they liked Tooling U-SME because it gives them opportunities to upgrade their personal skills portfolios and earn higher wages—while still allowing them to learn at their own pace and on their own time. Some of the most popular subjects include welding and machining, which are augmented by Saturday morning classes offered in the plant—just one of many examples of how e-learning complements hands-on training.

But while online courses and other initiatives have gone a long way toward shoring up its younger workers with the highly complex and technical job skills required for existing positions in the newly expanded plant, the 2010 expansion also created a bevy of *new* jobs that needed to be filled. So in addition to growing talent within the company, Siemens executives decided to make a commitment to grassroots training and development of the next generation of company employees by starting their own in-house apprenticeship program. Eager to get the ball rolling quickly, Siemens jointed Apprenticeship 2000, a program supported by several other manufacturers in the area who were motivated by the same skilled labor shortage that Siemens was experiencing. Launched in 1998 under the leadership of Blum USA, a manufacturer of kitchen cabinet and door hardware, and its CEO, Karl Ruedisser, Apprentice 2000 offered prospective employees the chance to enroll, *tuition-free,* in a three-and-a-half-year work-study program at the nearby Central

Piedmont Community College, earning both an associate degree in manufacturing technology *and* a guaranteed job at one of the member companies.

As I've seen over and over again in my work, one of the most challenging tasks setting up any new skills training program is finding and recruiting the *right* people. Siemens's experience echoed this. "Few young people around here had any idea of what went on in advanced manufacturing," Pamela said. "Those kids didn't have a clue about what opportunities are out there for them." This was compounded by "college for everyone" parents who were reluctant to allow their children to participate. Pamela "had to sell the program," through presentations at local high schools and plant tours for both students and their parents.

But Siemens doesn't just accept any applicant who expresses interest. Its program is highly selective, and begins with a thorough and rigorous screening process. The Siemens training team checks each candidate's school performance, speaks with teachers and counselors, and personally interviews every applicant. But that isn't the end of the audition. The individuals who pass through the initial screening test then have the opportunity to participate in four evening activities at the plant, where they are tested in measuring, math, and problem solving, as well as their ability to read prints. They are even given tests to assess their mechanical reasoning.

Those who pass the exams are then invited to a six-week summer pre-apprenticeship program (paid for entirely by Siemens) that includes classes at Central Piedmont Community College as well as a rotation through the different departments of the company's Charlotte Energy Hub. During those six weeks, apprentice candidates get a preview of what a day-to-day job at Siemens actually looks like, and what they would need to do to succeed over the next three and a half years. I like this a lot, as setting expectations up front is critical in designing any entry-level skills-building program. This also gives the Siemens supervisors an opportunity to carefully assess attitudes and aptitudes, work habits, and how each participant responds to supervision and instruction. Thanks to this careful pre-screening, program admittance rates of those who make it this far are high; on average, three-quarters of participants are accepted into the full three-and-a-half-year apprenticeship program.

While these standards are high, I think they are key to ensuring that those who gain acceptance to the program succeed. At the same time, the requirements lend the program a level of prestige that gives its graduates' résumés a competitive edge. The company's goal is to see every apprentice placed into a long-term career at the company, which is why they are so careful about choosing the people with not just the skills but the temperament, drive, motivation, and talent to flourish in their unique work environment.

Once the program kicks off in the early fall, each newly accepted apprentice is immediately paired with an experienced machinist or mechatronic mentor—an important feature given that, as I have mentioned before, mentors are a sponsoring company's best assurance that their apprentices will succeed. This is certainly the case at the Siemens Charlotte Energy Hub, where the training department and plant supervisors work together to select the best mentor candidates—people with both technical and interpersonal skills as well as some mentorship training.

At last count, there were seventeen apprentices in the pipeline, and the first of four cohorts was in its final year of training. The plant aims to enlarge the apprentice group to twenty-four and expand its outreach to area high schools. And that pool of qualified candidates is about to get even bigger, thanks to the new Energy Career Academy of Engineering being sponsored by Siemens and several other area employers, including Duke Energy, Piedmont Natural Gas, and Coca-Cola, at nearby Olympic High School.

At Siemens and companies like it, apprentices are seen as the future. "By the time our apprentices finish their training, they will understand the entire system," Pamela told me. "I see several of them stepping into leadership positions in coming years."

Ticket to Success

Rebeca Espinal was among the first class of apprentices at the Siemens Charlotte Energy Hub, and a sterling

184 | JOB U

example of how taking advantage of your company's on-the-job learning opportunities can bolster your career. She still remembers the day her high school counselor told her about apprenticeship openings at the newly expanded Siemens plant. Rebeca had just taken the SATs and had begun looking into a number of college programs, but none of them felt quite right to her. Suddenly she had a new opportunity to consider—one that had never entered her mind.

Having always dreamed of traveling abroad, Rebeca had been pondering a degree in international relations. As she put it to me, "I was always interested in learning about other countries, their history and geography." Thanks to her high grade point average, acceptance into a good program at a good school seemed likely. The costs of college, however, and the debts she'd have to take on were real concerns for Rebeca and her family, which is why the openings at Siemens captured her attention. "My counselor told me that an apprenticeship at Siemens would provide pay while I learned. And if everything worked out, I'd end up four years later with a good-paying job, an associate degree in mechatronics from our local community college, and no student loan debts." This sounded awfully good to Rebeca. So, when the Siemens team came to her high school to explain the program's details, Rebeca made a point of meeting them.

A few weeks later Rebeca, her father, and other interested students and parents found themselves in lockstep with a tour guide traversing the bustling floors of Siemens's gleaming new plant. It's an impressive place: quiet, clean, and filled with state-of-the-art machinery of a size and scale most people don't see very often. Its workers and tireless robots busy themselves with the intricate machining, welding, and wiring that eventually produces turbines and electric generators weighing up to six hundred tons. "For my dad, who's a machinist, this was a great field trip. He was *really* excited and supportive," she remembered.

Getting into the program, however, was no walk in the park. Rebeca had to submit her school course transcripts and attendance records, participate in interviews with key plant managers and the HR department, and take the placement test at Central Piedmont Community College. Upon passing through those screens, she and other candidates were then required to participate in the new Machining Apprentice Candidate summer internship program, which was designed primarily to give Siemens's watchful personnel a chance to evaluate the commitment and potential of each participant before deciding whether to grant them admission. If this selection process sounds unduly harsh, the fact is that the company would be investing nearly $160,000 in each apprentice's three-and-a-half-year training—and, may I repeat, *the company* would be making the $160,000 investment; not the apprentice or apprentice's family. But Rebeca passed with flying colors and in August 2011 she and several fellow interns were invited to sign on to the machining apprenticeship program. She was more than happy to accept.

That first year at Siemens turned out to alter the course her life dramatically, more so than if she had gone off to college. The day she stepped onto that factory floor, Rebeca stepped away from the world of teenage concerns and into the adult world of work, one of safety, precision, accountability, and teamwork. This was truly a learn-by-fire environment where even a tiny machining error could cost tens of thousands of dollars, and a major screwup could cost exponentially more. Serious business. Rebeca soon found herself enjoying spending two days each week in classes at CPCC, studying machining, physics, math, programming, English, the humanities, and other subjects. The rest of the workweek was spent doing hands-on work in one of the three main product areas of the plant: generators, steam turbines, and gas turbines. Over the past few years she and other apprentices have rotated through each unit, working under the wing of an experienced mentor.

"Working and studying at the same time wasn't easy," she told me. "And I'd be frustrated if I didn't understand what my mentors at work were teaching me. But they were patient and I managed to get through it all," which to Rebeca was a source of satisfaction. "I'd go home feeling that I'd learned something new and important. I was becoming more professional."

When I last spoke with Rebeca she was in the third year of her apprenticeship and was beginning to think about what her next move would be. That got me wondering: What lay ahead for this young woman whose initial aspiration had been to earn a college degree and build a career working and traveling around the world? I asked her what she saw for herself in the next four or five years. "At some point I plan to take courses at the University of NC in Charlotte that will lead to a mechanical engineering degree," she said. "With my associate degree from CPCC, I'll transfer in as a junior, and Siemens will reimburse tuition costs if I maintain good grades." Her years of production experience, combined with her associate degree, will put Rebeca on track for higher and higher advancement—and, in turn, open the door to more and more learning opportunities—within the company. And, as a mechanical engineer at a global business like Siemens, with operations all over the world, Rebeca will have all the overseas travel opportunities she could ever want—probably more than she would have had with an international relations degree. Her story just goes to show that in today and tomorrow's world of work, what makes a career is as much up to your imagination and willingness to take the time to invest in yourself and your education by whatever means available as it is about getting into the right school or getting a certain degree.

Skilling Up, Virtually

Siemens, Whole Foods Market, MGM Resorts International, STIHL, and American Infrastructure are great examples of organizations taking advantage of training and development to help skill up their workforces. But you don't have to wait for your company to offer programs like these to take advantage of all that learning has to offer. Opportunities exist widely in the world of online learning. In fact, the beauty of online courses is that they allow *anyone* to reboot, boost, or enhance their skill set—cheaply, easily, and anytime from anywhere. After all, not everyone can afford to take a protracted break out of their work life (what a friend of mine calls a "career sabbatical") to go back to school, and even a night or weekend course can be a major hardship for those with long or irregular workdays, and family or other obligations to deal with on their off hours. Fortunately, if you are one of these folks, online occupational learning makes it possible (and convenient and affordable) to hold on to your job and paycheck while learning something practical and new. Use it to advance your existing career or segue into something new.

A lot of online courses are offered through colleges and universities and can be found on their websites. For example, if you go to the website of one of America's larger postsecondary online providers, Miami-Dade College, you'll find a wealth of courses in areas such as construction, information technology, insurance, business management, green technology, languages, and real estate. The cost of online courses at Miami-Dade range from $20 to $600, and many will earn you a professional certification—the sort we talked about in chapter 3. And in this Miami-Dade is not unique. Many other community colleges and universities offer a huge range of online occupational and certificate courses that include some I'd never ever heard of. Minnesota West Community and Technical College, for example, offers a six-course certification program that trains people to install and maintain wind energy equipment. Be sure to do your research and find a reputable provider whose offer suits your need.

You may have heard about a recent breakthrough in educational technology that has dramatically expanded the scope and accessibility of online learning. The aptly named massive open online courses, or MOOCs, are indeed *massive* and *open* in the sense that they are available to everyone everywhere on the planet, and it's not uncommon for tens of thousands of people to sign up for a single course. Anyone wishing to audit a course (that is, take advantage of the learning without receiving academic credit) can do so free of charge and without academic prerequisites. Academic credits are often available for a fee that is usually far less than tuition for the traditional classroom version of the same course.

Throughout the book, we've visited places and met people who are revolutionizing the way we learn. MOOC environments are no different, other than the fact that the learning occurs in a virtual space rather than a physical one.

EdX (www.edx.org) is among the most celebrated of the MOOCs, providing access to courses offered by many of the Western world's most renowned universities, including MIT, Harvard, Stanford, the University of California at Berkeley, the University of Texas, Delft University of Technology, the Australian National University, and many more. Subject offerings run the academic gamut and give students a sense of "being there," with lecture videos, problem sets, virtual laboratories, selected reading material, and other pedagogical features. Another site to check out for online courses is www .coursera.org. Coursera also offers the convenience of a mobile app site. Initially working with Stanford University, Princeton, the University of Pennsylvania, and the University of Michigan, Coursera now has courses and content from more than one hundred worldwide educational institutions.

By taking elite and expensive educational experiences and making them available and affordable to the masses, MOOCs are playing a huge role in democratizing the entire system of elite education—and dealing "college for everyone" a blow in the process. Ongoing learning is a must, not a maybe, for all who want to invest in their career knowledge bank. Why rack up tens of thousands of dollars in debt to attend an elite university when you could get the same instruction online for free?

Advantages of MOOC Learning

- Bricks-and-mortar infrastructure is becoming costly for many providers.
- Open to people of all ages.
- Accessible from any location.

And Some Pitfalls

- Quality—you need to make sure the source is credible.
- Some people fear that MOOC learning may dilute the quality of higher education.
- Some people need to learn in a face-to-face environment and lack motivation and discipline to dedicate time to online learning. How do you like to learn?
- MOOCs have been under fire because a high percentage of enrollees sign up and then never finish the courses.

But to be clear, MOOCs aren't just offering the kinds of subjects you'd expect to find at universities, such as comparative literature or Greek mythology; these platforms offer a wealth of options in more practical and skills-based subjects ranging from chemistry and computer science to communication. Their offerings are so varied, in fact, that browsing EdX course descriptions has sparked my own personal interests on more than one occasion. It probably won't shock you to learn that one course that really grabbed me was an EdX Harvard course called Science and Cooking: From Haute Cuisine to Soft Matter Science.

Even if you aren't the least bit interested in watching "as chefs reveal the secrets behind some of their most famous culinary creations"[1] (to quote the course description), this course is a powerful example of how even the most hands-on skills can be taught virtually; after all, what could be more tangible than the smells, tastes, and textures of a coq au vin baking in the oven? The point is that no matter what your personal interests are—whether you're a car enthusiast, a robotics techie, or a foodie like me—if you visit the EdX website, I suspect you'll find at least several courses that will whet your appetite for further learning—and help you improve your performance on the job or move you up to the next stage or pay level in your line of work.

No matter what field you're in, what career you aspire to, and whether or not you work at a company like the ones profiled in this chapter, I'm willing to bet your employer offers opportunities to train on the job and undertake studies, whether it's a hands-on training program offered directly by your company, tuition reimbursement for continuing education or college courses, or access to platforms for online learning. So don't be afraid to walk into your human resources office or ask your supervisor or manager what's available, and if there's a particular course you want to take or skill you want to learn, there's no harm in asking if that learning experience can be reimbursed; after all, every dollar spent on your education and training not only enhances your marketability and earning power, but your employer's as well!

Keep in mind that these skilling-up opportunities aren't just for young people or those just starting out in the working world. The best thing about on-the-job learning is that it can be undertaken by anyone, at any stage of their life or careers, wishing to reboot or upgrade their skill sets—or even those wishing to completely re-invent or reimagine their careers.

Make Mastering Skills a Lifelong Vocation

Anyone who thinks they're too far along on their career path or that it's too late in life for them to seize the opportunities of a skills-based career, should be inspired by the examples of the many retirees or late-career professionals who decided to take their lives in new, more satisfying directions. Ken Gilbert is one of them. By the time I met him, Ken was three decades into his career in high-tech sales and marketing and management consulting. At age fifty-eight, however, after many years of business travel, meetings, and chasing corporate goals, he was ready for a change. "I thought about getting a master's degree and staying in the industry," he told me, "but if I was going to invest in something, I wanted it to be in something I would enjoy and be able to do for the rest of my life." Like many baby boomers, Ken didn't feel ready to retire, and didn't see why he couldn't extend his working career well beyond the traditional retirement age. And like many boomers, he also knew that if he wanted to live comfortably in his golden years, he'd need to find a way to supplement his pensions and savings with a steady paycheck.

Resolving to strike out on a new path, Ken looked into Boston's North Bennet Street School (NBSS), located just a few miles away from his New England home. Founded in 1881 as a social service organization primarily serving immigrants, the North Bennet Street School has a rich history of providing vocational and prevocational training. Like many of the educational institutions profiled throughout this book, NBSS follows a philosophy that hands-on skills are a necessary complement to academic conceptual skills. Today it attracts students from all over the country to its world-class full-time and continuing educational programs in "bench skills" that few other institutions offer: cabinet and furniture making, preservation carpentry, locksmithing, jewelry making and repair, bookbinding, even piano technician. Many NBSS graduates open craft-based businesses; others land prestigious and highly coveted positions in specialized fields. One preservation carpentry graduate, for example, launched his own custom home design company, while another, a bookbinding alumna, today is the rare book conservator for the Library of Congress. Yet another has become a luthier, getting very well paid to repair high-end violins and other stringed instruments. On my visits to the school I learned that current students and alumni are not just young people starting their careers; many students are late-career professionals, like Ken. It makes sense; after all, people in their forties and fifties and later are often in a great position to chuck what they've been doing and strike off in a new direction. In many cases their kids have left the nest, they've saved some money, their mortgages are paid off, and a spouse may be bringing in a reliable paycheck.

So when he learned about the opportunities offered at NBSS, Ken thought they seemed the perfect fit. He had the resources, the time, and the ability to go back to school and retrain as an artisan. Plus, working with his hands had always been one of his favorite pastimes—particularly woodworking and renovating an eighteenth-century house he owned. Ken has always liked making things, and he was good at it. So after talking with the school and considering his options, Ken decided to enroll in a two-year bookbinding program.

During those two years, Ken developed what he described to me as the three artisan essentials: "head, heart, and hands." And so it was that upon graduating from the program in 2010, Ken found himself, at age sixty, working full-time as a self-employed book conservator: making books from scratch, restoring old and rare books, repairing timeworn or damaged family heirloom volumes, and building leather-bound boxes in the shop he opened, Willow Bindery, in Shrewsbury, Massachusetts. Most of his customers today are book dealers and serious book collectors located all over the United States.

Now sixty-four, Ken Gilbert is engaged in a fulfilling occupation that he expects to continue for many more years. And he takes great satisfaction in what he does every day. "Restoring a cherished book, and then seeing the happy expression on the owner's face, is extremely gratifying."

That's Ken's story. What about yours? Are you at a place in life where you'd like to make a career shift? Perhaps your current line of work is being undermined by technological change. Or you're simply tired of selling insurance, churning out accounting statements, or dispensing legal advice. Maybe you've had enough of Power-Point presentations, Excel spreadsheets, conference calls, and windowless cubicles. Whatever the reason, for many it's a sign that now is the time to seize the opportunity to renew your working life by becoming good at something that gives you immense satisfaction while creating tangible value for others.

The fact is that no matter what you do or how much time you have banked in your current profession, there's nothing stopping you from doing a total 180 and taking your career in the opposite direction. Just ask Adam Liaw, a onetime lawyer recently turned master chef, who at midcareer, chose to shift gears and transition to an entirely new and exciting career opportunity—leaving life in an office behind him.

Adam is instantly recognizable by his trademark top-knot and neatly trimmed balboa-style beard. You may even recognize his name, if you are one of the foodies who has read his witty food and culture blog in the *Wall Street Journal*. But did you know that it wasn't until he was in his thirties that Adam realized he could build a secure and well-compensated career out of his underlying passion in food and flavors? Adam began his career as a lawyer—a path to which he'd invested more than a decade of traditional education and academic training. One day he decided to scrap it all and enter the *MasterChef Australia* reality TV contest, a reality cooking show that draws contestants from all over the country to compete for a spot in the televised finals.

The son of a Malaysian-born Chinese father and Singaporean-born English mother, Adam was part of a large extended family in which the children took turns cooking. "I learned a lot from my paternal grandmother, Kwei-Eng Chew, who lived with us," he told me. Grandparents often play a crucial role in shaping our passions; I know that from my own experience. But, unlike me, Adam followed a traditional academic pathway that eventually led to the world of food and kitchens. A standout scholar, he powered through an accelerated secondary school program and started university at age sixteen. By the time he was twenty-one he had graduated law school with a double degree. Yet despite his academic success, Adam was bored with classrooms and eager to enter the working world.

Upon graduating from law school, Adam landed a good job with a law firm, and eventually moved on to work for the Walt Disney Company, the world's largest media conglomerate. "Disney needed a Chinese-speaking lawyer [to practice in Japan]," he recollected, "and although I was not the most qualified person to apply, I had what it badly needed: a law degree and a reasonable proficiency in Chinese." (Even then skills were paying off for Adam—he had mastered a language.) Before he knew it, he was on a plane to Tokyo, where he lived and practiced media law for seven years. It was there that his appreciation for delicate flavors—and the skills required to prepare them—became part of his education. "Living in a foreign country forced me out of my comfort zone," he said. "Much inspiration came during trips to local supermarkets, where I found new ingredients. And with no ovens and limited space in ordinary Japanese kitchens, foreigners like me had to relearn basic cookery."

Then the global financial crisis hit and cast a cloud—a hiring freeze—over his plans to relocate to the States and transfer to Disney's Los Angeles headquarters. This unforeseen roadblock gave Adam an opportunity to think about where life was taking him. "I asked myself, 'Is it time for a change?' Pursuing a tip from friends, he decided on a whim to audition for *MasterChef Australia*. "I looked at this as a two-month holiday. That's how long I thought I might be on the show, if I got on at all," he said. "By then I figured that the hiring freeze at Disney in LA would end. I'd rent a place in the vineyards of South Australia, where I would write a book. And when the freeze was over, I'd go to LA and start working in media law again."

But as we've seen in countless stories throughout this book, our life journeys don't always go according to plan, and they often lead to destinations much different from the ones our younger selves envisioned. This was certainly the case for Adam, who was more surprised than anyone when he ended up winning viewers' hearts and judges' accolades, and taking the *MasterChef Australia* season two title in front of 4.2 million viewers in a finale that is still rated the number one nonsporting event in Australian television history. And that is how he found himself suddenly going from law to a new profession in food—a life that is worlds away from the career he thought he would have the day he entered college.

And all because Adam paused and took a step back to ask the question every young person must ask themselves at the start of their careers: Is this truly the path that most fully engages my interests, talents, and passions?

Over the past few years, Adam's answer led to cookbook deals, a regular column in the *Wall Street Journal*'s Scene Asia, and his own travel/food TV show, *Destination Flavor*. "It is a dream come true," he says, "and all the sweeter because I'm doing something I truly care about."

7

Bridging the Gap

During his 2012 State of the Union address, President Barack Obama made an impassioned plea calling on educators, industry, and communities alike to commit to working together to educate and build a more skilled workforce. To bring home the vast opportunity for economic, employment, and individual career success such collaboration can bring, he shared the story of a woman named Jackie Bray, a single mom from North Carolina who was laid off from her job as a mechanic. Bray's future was looking bleak, until Siemens opened a gas turbine factory in Charlotte, North Carolina, and formed a partnership with Central Piedmont Community College. Obama related how the company not only paid Jackie's tuition and helped the college design courses in laser and robotics training, it eventually hired her to help operate their plant.

"I want every American looking for work," President Obama continued, "to have the same opportunity as Jackie did. Join me in a national commitment to train two million Americans with skills that will lead directly to a job." He then called on Congress to give the nation's community colleges the resources they needed to "become community career centers—places that teach people skills that local businesses are looking for right now, from data management to high-tech manufacturing." He cited model partnerships between businesses like Siemens and community colleges in Charlotte, North Carolina; Orlando, Florida; and Louisville, Kentucky, that are already up and running.

From this speech, one thing is clear: The president is making skilling up a national imperative. And President Obama's commitment to closing the middle-skills gap in America isn't just oration; his words are fully bolstered by action. One concrete example is increased federal funding in the national budget for "high school redesign." More specifically, the U.S. government has now funded seven projects through a $100 million (spanning four years) grant program called Youth CareerConnect that aims to redesign the public high schools to make them more responsive to local economic needs. Among a number of elements, the program calls for partnership with local industry—the key ingredient of many of the successful programs you'll read about in the pages ahead.

President Obama is not alone in acknowledging the importance of education pathways that end in solid careers. Over the past few years, the subject of how to reintroduce and reinvigorate skills-based education and training in our nation's secondary and postsecondary schools has continually been appearing as cover stories in major magazines and news programs, opinion pieces in major newspapers, and the subject of ongoing discussions around kitchen tables, on college campuses, in corporate boardrooms, and across the blogosphere. These conversations suggest we are on the cusp of a skills-based revolution, and the time is ripe for companies, schools, and communities to start taking action to bridge the gap from well-meaning rhetoric to real-world solutions.

So what actions do educators, employers, and the government need to take to spark a successful resurgence of skills education? The same ones required of anyone who wants to enact sweeping social change. First and foremost is recognizing that great things happen when people are open to listening, communicating, and working together to contribute their expertise and resources toward a common good.

Second is acknowledging that a piecemeal approach to solving this economic and employment challenge no longer works—that employers, educators, and communities alike need to partner on a grander scale than ever before. Because only once educators truly understand the practical and workplace skills that local employers need and are willing to adapt their curricula to those requirements, when employers engage with schools and students to help *them* understand the skills they need and are then willing to take an active role in fostering those skills, *and* when communities and governments create business conditions that give employers tangible incentives to employ newly skilled workers will we see true innovation and change in a system that has been stagnant for far too long.

The good news is that these things are starting to happen. Right now, industry leaders, astute employers, educators, and policy makers across the country and across the globe are coming together to drive innovation and change in education and advance the cause of skills-based careers.

Momentum is building; the skills-based opportunities of today and tomorrow can and will exist in a variety of partnerships between school and industry, entrepreneurism and philanthropy, employers and educators, and law and policy makers from the federal level down through to your local municipality.

I've always felt that one of America's great strengths is its ability to craft cross-sector partnerships like these. In the pages ahead, I will profile a number of partnerships and initiatives that hold great promise for closing the skills gap, reinventing the relationship between school and work, and redefining what successful career pathways look like. These initiatives all share the same goal: to help people gain a foothold in the world of work and position them for a sustainable career and a sound economic future.

Schools and Industry Partnerships: A Story of Innovation in Education

The first of these initiatives is P-TECH, or Pathways in Technology Early College High School, a high school in

Brooklyn. A radical departure from your traditional high school, P-TECH is a collaborative partnership between the New York City Department of Education, the City University of New York, and one of the world's most recognized corporations, IBM, creator of thousands of new tech jobs each year around the globe. P-TECH aims to equip high school students with the knowledge and core practical and workplace skills to better prepare them to land and succeed in entry-level employment with the world's leading technology companies or in the IT industry. By extending traditional high school beyond grade twelve to grade fourteen, providing a seamless integration of high school and college courses over six years, P-TECH graduates students with both a high school diploma and an in-demand associate in applied science degree in the information technology field.

P-TECH, which opened its doors in September 2011, follows a philosophy articulated by former Mayor Michael Bloomberg in his 2008 State of the City speech: "Career and technical education has been seen as an educational dead end. We're going to change that. College isn't for everyone, but education is."

Indeed, like many high schools across the country, New York City public high schools have long had plenty of room for improvement. As of 2010, only 65 percent of New York City high school students were graduating, and of those who did, less than 40 percent were judged prepared to pursue a career or postsecondary education.[1] While P-TECH's first class of students has now finished year three, they are showing remarkable progress that will more than likely shatter these disappointing results. While most big-city high schools struggle with truancy, high levels of dropouts, and low achievement, since its opening, P-TECH has had a 97 percent attendance rate and good scores on standardized tests.

What accounts for this success?

For one, P-TECH breaks the traditional four-year high school model; the additional two years of instruction, along with extended hours and an extended school year, allow the instructors to give greater time and attention to college and career readiness and to provide hands-on workplace experience through internships and cooperative learning opportunities primarily with IBM, as well as with other local technology companies. And because the school focuses on mastery over seat time, high school and college classes are integrated seamlessly; rather than students completing four years of high school, followed by two years of college, most students are earning college credits while still in the traditional high school phase of their six-year experience. By the beginning of the eleventh grade, 25 percent of the first class of P-TECH students had completed all of their high school requirements. In fact, 50 percent of eleventh graders had at least ten college credits midyear, and by year-end, one-third of the eleventh graders will have completed a full year of college.

Incentives and supports are key. Every student who

successfully completes the six-year program with an AAS degree is "first in line" for jobs at IBM. Moreover, by providing a seamless integration of high school and college classes with individualized support for students, P-TECH ensures that students are fully prepared to participate in college classes upon graduating rather than walking into their first-year classroom to find that remediation is required. In other words, these additional two years not only permit students to complete a two-year college degree; they also instill the skills, motivation, and confidence that come with being actively engaged and involved in their own learning.

Another reason for P-TECH's high success rate is the fact that its curriculum integrates STEM-oriented (science, technology, engineering, and math) subject matter with specific employability skills that are widely acknowledged to be critical elements to workplace success, including problem solving, working with teams, effectiveness in making presentations, and analytical thinking. Moreover, these practical skills are embedded in every class across the curriculum, whether it is algebra, English, or physics.

Most coursework and lessons are wrapped in real-life situations designed to enhance students' job-readiness; teamwork is emphasized throughout, with students working on semester-long class projects that simulate projects they might someday encounter in the real-world workplace. As just one example, in a class called virtual enterprise, students apply for positions such as CEO and CFO and other key roles you'd find in a real-world business, then work together to set project goals, craft plans and strategies for reaching those goals, and then present their results.

Every P-TECH student has an IBM mentor who provides academic and career guidance—another factor in supporting P-TECH graduates' high performance academically and then later in the workforce. Mentoring is a key part of a larger workplace learning umbrella that includes site visits, hands-on projects, job shadowing, and skills-based paid internships. Mentors visit the school regularly to meet with their student mentees, work with them and their teachers on projects, and engage with other mentors. And because of the school's location and the busy schedules of mentors, IBM also supports mentor and student communication through an online platform. To date, hundreds of IBM employees have volunteered as mentors, creating a win-win situation by which young students benefit from the encouragement and feedback of experienced professionals, and employees enjoy meaningful volunteer opportunities that build company engagement and pride. As Stanley S. Litow, IBM's vice president of corporate citizenship and corporate affairs, president of the IBM International Foundation, and a leading figure in launching the P-TECH school model, told me, "Our employees are very excited about having an opportunity to make a big difference in young peoples' lives."

Finally, P-TECH, through its founding principal,

Rashid Ferrod Davis, has created a culture of excellence. At IBM, culture is everything, and this is a big part of what has enabled the company to continue to thrive even as its core business has evolved from time clocks to laptops to advanced computing services. At P-TECH, every teacher, staff member, and partner believes that each student can succeed—and that belief is then transferred to each student. Remember that the students at P-TECH attend a longer school day and school year, and often work longer and harder than their peers at traditional high schools. They are inspired to do so by the adults around them, by their fellow students, and by their belief in themselves.

The cost for earning an associate degree in applied science at P-TECH is the same as the cost of attending a traditional public high school—which is to say, completely free. Incredibly, P-TECH costs no more than a traditional high school to operate, and its teachers, while carefully handpicked by the principal, are paid on par with a regular high school teacher salary. Unlike that at many top-notch high schools, its enrollment is not limited to children living in affluent districts. To the contrary, P-TECH is located in a disadvantaged neighborhood and is available to all on an open admissions basis—without testing or grade requirements.

As innovative as its methods may be, the concept of focused academies like P-TECH are not entirely new. In fact, their success within the New York City school system goes back more than seventy years. Aviation High

School is one example. Located in Queens, it has been offering its students rigorous training in aircraft maintenance since 1936 and is rated among the country's best high schools. Because the school's programs are certified by the U.S. Federal Aviation Administration, Aviation High's graduates can sit for FAA certification exams without further qualifications or training, so they are ready to enter the industry when they walk out the door. And like P-TECH, Aviation High has negligible attendance problems; it graduates 88 percent of its students, nearly 80 percent of whom go on to postsecondary education, where many major in aeronautics and engineering.

One can only imagine how our world would change if every high school produced work-ready, college-ready graduates at that rate. Youth unemployment, crime, and dependency would drop like a rock. Hand wringing over the demise of the middle class would end. Our companies would once again be truly competitive in a global economy. The benefits for society are limitless.

But are programs like P-TECH scalable? True, P-TECH has received lots of positive attention in the media and education circles, yet it is only one small school, and the first class of students is yet to graduate (2015). But IBM never intended for P-TECH to be a single jewel in Brooklyn, helping only a small number of young people; IBM leaders, along with the company's partners, have always seen system-wide reform as the long-term goal. Indeed, the model was designed to be sustainable, replicable, scalable, and easily adoptable by other school systems.

Of course, the more this model spreads, the more questions there will be to be answered and the more issues there will be to overcome: Will its graduates be as competent and employable five or ten years down the road as they are at the entry level? Can the P-TECH model be applied successfully to other student populations and in a variety of industries?

Although only time will tell, early signs of success can be seen in several tangible ways. For one, replication of the P-TECH model is already well under way. In 2012, just one year after P-TECH opened, Chicago mayor Rahm Emanuel replicated the model in five Early College STEM schools, with IBM serving as lead industry partner for one (the Sarah E. Goode STEM Academy), and Cisco, Microsoft, Motorola, and Verizon shepherding the other four. The mayor's willingness to try something radically different was understandable given that a shocking 40 percent of Chicago's high school starters were failing to graduate. The resulting cost to the city—in terms of welfare and unemployment checks, lost tax revenues, crime, and squandered human potential—was truly mind-boggling, and the school system's failure to produce employable workers was hamstringing the city's effort to attract new businesses.

In addition to P-TECH, New York City has replicated the model in two schools that opened in 2013. Two more opened in 2014, and New York governor Andrew Cuomo said he would fund sixteen P-TECH schools statewide—one in each of the state's economic development districts—in 2015. These will be industry-focused institutions that are committed to producing graduates for in-demand fields, including IT, health care, and advanced manufacturing. IBM is serving as lead industry partner for one school, Excelsior Academy, in Newburgh, New York, which is near the company's large manufacturing plants, and is providing leadership for all the schools through its participation in the governor's steering committee. Each school will have its own set of district, higher education, and corporate collaborators. In addition, Governor Cuomo put forth a program under which the top 10 percent of New York State students who pursue STEM careers over five or more years within the state will enjoy free tuition at any City University of New York or State University of New York campus. Following on the heels of Governor Cuomo's announcement, Connecticut governor Dannel Malloy announced that his state, too, will replicate the model. Like in New York, IBM will lead one school, Norwalk Early College Academy, which will open its doors in 2014, and will provide guidance over the state's P-TECH network of schools.

High youth unemployment and our skills gap will not go away by themselves; we need to do something about them. Reforms to traditional schools and to our extensive vocational education system will certainly help, but to create game-changing improvements we need to experiment with radically different and boldly innovative models. Luckily, P-TECH is just one of several examples of new pioneering partnerships aimed at shaking up education. Let's read about some others.

||||||||||||||||||||||||||||||||||||||||||||||||||||||||||||||||||||||||||||||||||||||||||||||||

PROGRAM HIGHLIGHT:

CULTURE AND CURRICULUM

The success of P-TECH and programs like it prove that a culture of high achievement and a seamless high school and college curriculum that is engaging and relevant tackles the issues of truancy, dropouts, and low achievement that plague many traditional high schools.

||||||||||||||||||||||||||||||||||||||||||||||||||||||||||||||||||||||||||||||||||||||||||||||||

Entrepreneurial Partnerships: Connecting to High-Tech Jobs

What is the path to a career in a *Fortune* 500 company? Contrary to what you might think, it's not only an MBA from a prestigious business school or university. Graduates of the next program I describe have ended up working at companies such as Google, Time Warner, and AT&T. Some have even ended up working at NASA.

Year Up is a private nonprofit organization that aims to provide disadvantaged young adults with the skills, experience, and support they need to realize their potential through solid careers and/or higher education. Year Up is the brainchild of founder and CEO Gerald Chertavian, who established the organization in Boston in 2000. Yet the seeds of Chertavian's vision for Year Up were planted many years before, when he volunteered as a Big Brother and was troubled by what he saw as an opportunity divide—a barrier to success for his ten-year-old "Little Brother" and millions like him. As Gerald would later write in his book *A Year Up*:

> I thought it was so wrong that the opportunities he had access to in life could be limited due to things like his zip code, the color of his skin, the bank balance of his mother, or the school system he attended. We are wasting so much talent in a country where we have none to waste.[2]

Research told Gerald that there were about three million "disconnected" young adults in the United States—people who were neither working, in postsecondary education, nor serving in the armed forces. By 2014 that number had grown to 6.7 million, a shocking 15 percent of all eighteen- to twenty-four-year-old Americans. Most had high school diplomas or the equivalent. A few had had some college training. But none had achieved economic self-sufficiency nor secured a foothold in the world of work.

Gerald Chertavian wanted to help these people out of this socioeconomic quagmire by building an organization that would first teach these individuals the skills they would need in white-collar urban jobs, then place them as interns with local companies and support their development through mentoring and regular feedback. The result was the yearlong skilling-up program appropriately named Year Up.

To be eligible to join Year Up, you need to be a young adult between eighteen and twenty-four years of age, be a high school graduate or a GED holder, and be of low to moderate income. The program requires you to be available five days a week for the full year of the program. But the most important eligibility criterion is that you must be highly motivated to learn new technical and professional skills.

My introduction to Year Up and its founder was through a case study written by Harvard professor Allen Grossman. Upon reading the case study I thought, "Gerald Chertavian is doing in America what I've been doing in Australia—connecting young people to the workplace—but in a different way." I immediately knew I wanted to meet him and learn more.

I first met Gerald at his Boston office in 2011. Both businesslike and charismatic, Gerald was clearly passionate about his mission. After our initial meeting Gerald suggested that the best way to understand his organization fully was to go out and talk to some of its young participants. That was when Heeyoon Chang Slater, the director of strategic program pilots, introduced me to two incredible young people: Victor and Tyriek.

Both were in the final week of their in-house training

and about to be placed for six months as interns with local partner companies. They were both cordial and animated, and professionally dressed, in keeping with Year Up's obligatory professional attire code. And they were more than happy to talk to me at length about the program, what it meant to them, and how it was changing their future outlooks for the better. As they described their experience, one thing couldn't have been more clear: Both were grateful for the structure, discipline, and high expectations that Year Up was introducing into their lives.

During the first six-month block of the yearlong program, they explained, students are taught basic IT and financial skills in a classroom-based environment, where they earn up to eighteen college credits through an extensive community college network that includes Atlanta Metropolitan State College, Baltimore City Community College, Bellevue College, Cambridge College, City College of San Francisco, Community College of Rhode Island, Foothill College, Harold Washington College, Miami-Dade College, Northern Virginia Community College, Peirce College, and others. They also receive training in the soft skills that so many of the program's partners are looking for in employees: how to communicate through emails and presentations, work on teams, manage their time, negotiate, resolve conflicts, give a proper handshake, and so forth—little things that most of us take for granted. Through it all they are imbued with Year Up's values of personal accountability, honesty, hard work, learning, and respect for others.

The second six-month block of the program gives every student an opportunity to apply their knowledge through an internship with one of the organization's corporate partners, many of which are technology companies, financial services firms, retail and service industry firms, or health care facilities. They include the American Cancer Society, Baxter International, Bain Capital, American Express, Brooks Running, Deloitte, eBay, Gap, Hilton Worldwide, LinkedIn, and Salesforce.com, to name a few, and are located in Atlanta, Baltimore, Boston, Chicago, Miami, New York City, Philadelphia, Providence, Puget Sound/Seattle, and the San Francisco Bay Area.

After completing the program, Victor and Tyriek were placed as interns with Deutsche Bank, where they receive a biweekly stipend of around $150 per week. Of course, that sum doesn't cover their full living expenses—many of the students have part-time or evening jobs to get by— but it certainly helps pay the bills, and it doesn't count the incalculable value the experience brings to their professional networks and résumés. The stipend is subject to good performance bonuses (though also may be reduced in the event of unprofessional behavior, indifferent work, or tardiness)—and is a good way to reinforce standards and accountability.

Gerald Chertavian's formula for connecting the disconnected is clearly succeeding. Seventy percent of students finish the program, and of those, 85 percent are employed or in full-time postsecondary schooling within four months of graduation. Starting annual salaries are usually around $30,000 with benefits. That's not a mountain of money, but it's respectable and livable compensation for unseasoned entry-level employees with no more than high school diplomas, and for many, it provides just the foothold in the adult world of work they need to break the cycle of joblessness and poverty that has ensnared so many of their peers. And while Year Up grads may initially find themselves on the first rung of the career ladder, many go on to get promoted to higher and higher rungs. Compared to costly government job training programs that serve the same disconnected population, those are fabulous results.

These days, Gerald Chertavian spends most of his time raising money for the program, spreading the success of Year Up, building relationships with businesses and local community colleges, and scaling up the enterprise, with impressive results. Thanks to grants from both individual and corporate contributors, since its 2000 launch in Boston, Year Up has replicated its model across the country, and the list of Year Up corporate partners has grown to include Microsoft, Twitter, the National Aquarium, the Boston Children's Hospital, and the American Red Cross.

More than 8,500 eighteen- to twenty-year-olds have been served since the program's launch, and as of early 2014, 5,200 had completed the full year satisfactorily.

Today thousands of Year Up alumni can be found in well-paying white-collar jobs in businesses nationwide. People like Paola Walter, who only a few years after graduating from Year Up is a senior fund accountant at State Street. Or Jay Hammonds, who is in executive support at Facebook, and who, after a few promotions, is working his way to becoming an IT executive. There are countless others like them. Paola's words summed up the refrain I heard from many of these young graduates when she told me that "choosing to not press on with college and join Year Up was the best decision I have ever made."

PROGRAM HIGHLIGHT: ANYTHING IS POSSIBLE

Year Up teaches that if you bring attributes such as passion, determination, reliability, and resilience to any education or work situation, regardless of your circumstance or the barriers you faced getting to the starting line, good people and employers will give you a go.

Higher Education Partnerships: Where Harvard U Meets Job U

Some of the nation's most prestigious colleges are pioneering new and innovative collaborations among education, government, and industry. Since 2011, the research-driven

U.S. Competitiveness Project at Harvard Business School has worked to identify practical steps that policy makers and especially business leaders can take to strengthen the U.S. economy—and closing the skills gap is one of them. Led by Harvard professors and strategy experts Michael Porter and Jan Rivkin, the project aims specifically to devise ways of keeping the U.S. economy successful on a global scale as well as capable of supporting high and rising living standards for Americans. "Many of the issues we see in America today—jobs pressure, flat real household incomes, stagnant standards of living—arise because we as a nation have not yet addressed crucial drivers of competitiveness," said Jan Rivkin. "The project focuses on identifying and strengthening those drivers so that we can secure opportunity for the current and next generation of Americans."

One aspect of the project centers on closing the middle-skills gap, which Professors Porter and Rivkin see as vital to U.S. economic competitiveness. In partnership with Accenture and Burning Glass, HBS faculty are working on identifying the true scope of the gap in the United States, with research emphasizing concrete steps that can be taken to bridge the gap between supply and demand for middle skills. "We believe business can and must play a role in closing skills gaps," said Rivkin.

In New York, the local HBS alumni club has answered this call for action. Their efforts are small in size at the moment, but they have great potential to engage other business leaders in taking a stance against the skills gap. Distinguished HBS alumni Bruce Bockmann and Richard Kane, along with a team from the club, have embraced U.S. competitiveness research since early 2012. Their skills-gap project is leading the charge to connect education to jobs on the local level, with initial focus on health care and early stage IT.

Their approach casts the alumni in the role of "network integrators," responsible for developing meaningful connections between corporate, education, and government professionals who do not normally communicate effectively but are facing the same problems. According to Bockmann and Kane, the Harvard Business School Club of New York "has been able, in a pilot approach, to identify where collaboration is needed, identify the appropriate parties, and see to it that they meet, understand each other, and focus on the solutions." The network integrator model, in other words, connects the dots between the supply and demand sides of the skills gap by seeing to it that the business sector communicates its middle-skills needs to the community colleges. This, in turn, prompts community colleges to establish new curricula and new programs to generate graduates with those very skills.

The early stage technology company initiative is one of the first efforts in this direction and has already generated curriculum modifications that include greater focus on much-needed programming skills as well as better soft skills instruction. One "skill" required by most employers is job experience, which, of course, few students have. To fill that gap, the HBSCNY is stressing the need for more internship programs, both paid and unpaid. The club has agreed to fund a stipend program for students who need paying jobs while completing their internships at companies that cannot afford to compensate them. One such student, originally from Bangladesh, completed a three-month internship and immediately received a job offer and stock in the company. The result has been more jobs for community college students who never dreamed of such opportunities, and at the same time, a new source of talent for early-stage companies that could not afford to compete with larger and more mature companies for computer science majors from big universities.

The network integrator model offers clear benefits to both colleges and businesses, as well as to the thriving workforce that it will help to create. If it continues to prove successful in New York, it could be rolled out nationally and internationally through the Harvard network. Efforts such as these have the potential to not only increase U.S. economic competitiveness, but to also change the face of careers in this country.

Philanthropic Partnerships: Going from Unemployed to Employable

The International Labor Organization puts the number of jobless people in the world at nearly two hundred million, and most of the unemployed are young. These people may have failed to make a smooth school-to-work transition or been laid off from a job in a declining industry, displaced by outsourcing and automation, or marginalized for some other reason. The good news is that these staggering numbers represent an enormous untapped pool of potential talent. Yet the leap from unemployment to the world of work must seem impossible for many long-term unemployed. It is, in short, a vicious cycle.

Luckily, businesses and philanthropies around the world are coming together to tackle this problem because they understand it's an issue that affects everyone. New Recruits, the initiative I describe next, was founded in my home country of Australia and has the potential to be duplicated and replicated in any community around the globe. This particular program aims to reengage the disengaged and models a new form of partnership with philanthropy and industry; it is a four-week-long *pre*-apprenticeship/traineeship course designed to give people a jump-start into skilled careers and well-paying jobs. It also happens to be one that I myself cofounded. I saw a need and found a way to address it.

Most apprenticeship and training programs aimed at assisting people in the school-to-work transition that I have worked with last one to four years and enroll around six hundred to seven hundred people annually. I'd always wanted to design and implement a fundamental skills program that would prepare people to enter the pipeline on a much faster time frame and in much greater numbers. Initially, I thought that government would be the proper sponsor of such a program, but I soon realized that while governments have long experimented with policies and incentives to entice employers to hire on long-term unemployed people, the results have generally been mixed. More often than not, when the funding stops, so do the jobs.

This is not entirely surprising, given that governments typically face obstacles ranging from bureaucratic red tape to bipartisan discord to pressure on allocation of limited funds. Moreover, the wheels of government often take a long time to turn—time that many young people do not have. So when I set out to design a program to help long-term unemployed workers shore up their skill sets and reengage with the working world, I figured that private philanthropy was a better place to start.

In 2012, I first discussed this idea with Skilling Australia Foundation chairman Frederick Maddern OBE, an expert so knowledgeable on matters of community engagement, government, and employment that he received the high honor of an Order of the British Empire for his services in these areas. Immediately seeing the need for a program like the one I was describing, Fred, a man who never tolerates procrastination, gave me this advice: "Nick, do it, and do it now!" So I did.

Together with my associate Joanne Gedge (with whom I have worked on several large international consultancies and research assignments, including the development of a mentoring framework, a supply-side review for Singapore's Workforce Development Agency, and a vocational international benchmarking study covering the United States, Singapore, New Zealand, the United Kingdom, Australia, and Germany), I assembled an all-star team of specialist researchers. Our first task was to interview employers and jobless young people and gather whatever data we could find on unemployed and disengaged youth. After poring through reams of research, we concluded our initial hypothesis to have been spot-on: Our data confirmed that the primary reasons so many young people have difficulty entering the labor market are both a lack of work-relevant skills and credentials, and poor information about careers. Thus, our program would need to address both of these barriers in concert.

A week after completing our research I found myself in the New York City offices of the Citi Foundation, which works to promote economic progress in communities around the world and focuses on initiatives that expand financial inclusion. It was there I met with Jasmine Thomas, a program officer at the foundation. Jasmine was the perfect person to discuss my ideas with, as she directs the foundation's international investments and specifically their new Youth Economic Opportunities portfolio. It became clear during our conversations that the Citi Foundation believes that investing in young people is critical in order to set them and their communities on the path toward economic success. Jasmine described the importance of the challenge before us: "In a globalizing world, it is increasingly hard to grasp how employment and entrepreneurship pipelines will be developed without better ideas, targeted investments, and more inclusive models that directly position young people to access as well as create new economic opportunities for themselves and their communities."

Jasmine and I were on the same wavelength. We both agreed that the target age group on which we should focus on was seventeen- to twenty-four-year-olds, since this group is the hardest hit by unemployment (in Australia, recent statistics indicated that the unemployment rate among youth ages fifteen to nineteen was as high as 40.7 percent in certain regions), and most in need of a plan to get them on the right track. Moreover, due to their age, this was the group most lacking in real on-the-job experience and training.

With funding and support from the Citi Foundation, and working in partnership with the Citi Australia team, the program quickly moved from concept into reality. Our 120 initial participants were mostly young people from lower socioeconomic backgrounds who had a family history of long-term underemployment or disengagement and/or lacked the academic background or basic educational qualifications necessary to secure and then keep full-time employment.

The program begins with a four-week intensive phase that combines hands-on vocational training, job-readiness workshops, and mentoring. Phase one of the program focuses on skills needed for a job in Australia's robust hospitality and tourism industry, such as food preparation and presentation, occupational health and safety, and kitchen operations (though we plan to eventually expand the scope to other industries). We even teach them to make a first-rate espresso!

Beyond these basic technical skills, recruits learn the attitudes and work habits crucial for success in the workplace, such as the importance of showing up on time and giving every assignment their best shot—things that the rest of us pick up from the positive adult role models that many disadvantaged young people lack. And so we try to make up for that. For me, this is critically important. And so on the first day we acquaint them with the program's four values—opportunity, pride, independence, and accountability—and help them to understand how these values relate to their job and career aspirations.

Over the course of the four weeks, each recruit develops an action plan and spends a day or two at a variety of work sites to get a feel for what kind of career and work environment is most personally suitable. At the end of week four, our recruits receive a Certificate 1 in Vocational Preparation, which in the Australian system is a portable, nationally recognized qualification that serves as evidence to any would-be employer that the individual has completed a course of vocational preparation and/or credits toward their apprenticeship. Of course, Certificate 1 and apprenticeship credits are only the first rung on the skills ladder, but both put job seekers well ahead of where they were, and both give them a leg up on the competition for entry-level jobs.

At that point we place our certificate holders with one of the hundreds of companies in the Skilling Australia Foundation network, and assign a mentor to each. Importantly, those employers, in industries including tourism, hospitality, general business, and service, have been with the program since its inception and had a hand in its design.

The best way to describe this program's initial results is through the story of one of its early participants. Memuna, now twenty-three, was born in Sierra Leone. When war broke out, her parents took their two-year-old daughter to live with her grandmother in Guinea, where, like me, she learned the joys of cooking at her grandmother's apron strings. Upon her seventeenth birthday, she emigrated from Guinea to Australia, where she struggled to gain an education. "My father brought me to this new country in 2008," she said. "I only knew my mother tongue and the French I had learned in school, so it was hard at first. I spent a year in an intensive English language program before completing secondary school. Later I started a college course but something was missing. I wanted to cook."

So in 2013 she joined the New Recruits program and was successfully placed as a beginning apprentice in a busy kitchen in Sydney. I recently asked Memuna how things were progressing.

"I am so excited to have a cooking apprenticeship at

a restaurant where the chili and coriander remind me of my grandmother cooking for our big family," she told me. "The program put me on track after I found studies weren't for me. I undertook work experience in a kitchen as a high school student, and I really liked it. The chef there asked me to whip some cream. I'd never done that before, and I was amazed at what I created—turning a liquid into this nice fluffy stuff! I knew then I wanted to be a chef."

Memuna is now mastering the art of preparation and presentation of cuisine—all skills she will require and hone as she progresses in her apprenticeship. She is already looking forward to traveling the world, tasting new things, and experiencing new environments where familiar ingredients are used in different ways. Her favorite dish? Chicken quesadillas.

The New Recruits program is only an initial step in beginning to solve the enormous youth unemployment crisis, but it is a step—and one that will hopefully serve as a model to others who wish to develop skill-building programs or partnerships in their own communities or businesses. At the time of this writing, more than one hundred new recruits had completed the four-week pre-employment training and more than 80 percent had gained employment or enrolled in further studies. More cohorts were expected to graduate by the end of the calendar year. It's only a start, but it's changing each of those lives for the better. When I think about what we're doing, I like to think of the old story about the child who was walking with her father along the beach as the tide rolled out, stranding thousands of starfish. Seeing one at her feet, she picked it up and tossed it back into the surf. "Don't waste your time," said her father. "There are thousands of stranded starfish on the beach. Saving one doesn't matter."

"It matters to that one," she replied.

And don't forget that engaging unemployed people in the workforce also matters to the communities in which they live. I personally feel satisfaction that each young person we launch into a productive life is one less welfare recipient, one more taxpayer, and one more consumer of other people's goods and services. When one person's economic situation is improved, we all win. That's how we strengthen our communities and fuel economies: one person at a time.

PROGRAM HIGHLIGHT:
FOCUS ON FOUNDATION SKILLS

We like to remind our program participants to think not only about the skills they need to land a job, but also the skills they need to *keep* a job. These are skills modern employers look for, and they are ones that can't necessarily be learned in a classroom, such as the ability to communicate and work well with others.

Community Partnerships: Driving Success Through Large-Scale Collaboration

In researching this book, I found there to be two common ingredients to all programs that are succeeding in skilling up young people and creating employment opportunities in their communities: collaboration and a passion for improving the lives and fortunes of one's neighbors. Those two ingredients may be the elements that separate successful development programs from all the rest.

A story taking place in South Carolina, and Pickens County in particular, is probably the best example of the power of large-scale collaboration between several powerful forces: employers, educators, economic developers, government, and community. Over the past decade, South Carolina has experienced an economic renaissance of a sort. Up until the late 1990s, textiles had been the state's main industry—what automobiles had once been to Michigan. By the turn of the century, however, most of the industry, undercut by competition from Mexico, India, Pakistan, Sri Lanka, China, and Vietnam, had evaporated, shutting down mills and leaving thousands of people unemployed.

This bleak situation began to reverse itself in the mid-1990s as the area's climate and business environment began to attract global companies such as GE Aviation and BMW. When most of the manufacturing sector in the United States was bleeding manufacturing jobs,

South Carolina was doing the opposite. From early 2011 to mid-2012 alone, more than two hundred manufacturing firms committed to projects that would potentially produce over twenty-four thousand new jobs in the state. And by 2014, 221,800 South Carolinians—16.4 percent of the workforce—were employed by one of the state's five thousand manufacturing firms, a workforce percentage that far exceeded the U.S. average of 9 percent (and one that was remarkable for a state with an agricultural heritage).

How did this happen? Surely it wasn't just the lure of global business; like every other state, South Carolina and its economic development districts had long tried to attract new enterprises—particularly manufacturers—with the standard menu selection: a right-to-work law, multiyear tax breaks, low living costs, and promises of infrastructure improvements. Yet those enticements (or as some might call them "daily specials") put South Carolina no further ahead than its competitors, given that every state and every development agency was offering the same. No, what differentiated South Carolina was the decision to make a commitment to developing a skilled workforce.

If it sounds far-fetched that a commitment to skilling up the workforce would be enough to lure businesses to the state, keep in mind that many of the prospective employers scouting the area were European companies whose operations depended on a labor force highly skilled in advanced manufacturing. So when, with a big push from the South Carolina Chamber of Commerce, state legislators put together a coordinated initiative to actually *develop and build* a human resources pool with the skills companies badly needed, employers responded with enthusiasm. A key part of the plan to attract employers to their part of the sunny South was to boost the number of apprentice positions offered by companies around the state, and boost them they did; since 2007 the number of apprentice positions in South Carolina has grown six-fold, and by early 2014, nearly ten thousand individuals were either working as apprentices or had completed their programs and been certified. It's worth noting that a surprising number of these apprentices are actually college graduates who had not found meaningful entry-level employment in their chosen academic fields of study and learned that real-world work experience could launch their working lives and open the door to career opportunities.

Meanwhile, the number of sponsoring employers exploded from 90 to 660, in part thanks to the state's offer of a $1,000 annual tax credit per apprentice. These sorts of sums may not seem like much for a large multinational corporation, but they are, in my experience, powerful incentives for employers, who put the money toward the costs of training an apprentice. Remarkably, this progress did not require an army of government agency personnel or huge taxpayer outlays.

But the tax break is far from the only measure South Carolina's government and lawmakers have taken to support the state's successful skills-training programs. The legislation that enabled the employer tax credit also provided funding for a small state-run agency dubbed Apprenticeship Carolina™, which aims to provide employers with the information and technical assistance they need to create apprenticeship programs in their organizations. This new agency was not housed in the state government bureaucracy, but inside the Economic Development and Workforce Competitiveness Division of the respected sixteen-campus SC Technical College System, where business acumen and commercial expertise are readily available. Program consultants need to be in tune with regional employers and their needs, and be able to form solid working relationships with people at all levels of organizations.

Apprenticeship Carolina consists of six well-versed apprenticeship consultants, all of whom are assigned to a set of counties, statewide. The operation is headed up by its charismatic, hands-on director Brad Neese. Brad and his team of consultants provide information on the employer benefits and obligations that go with registered apprenticeships, and help companies with the paperwork they must complete to register their programs with the U.S. Department of Labor.[3] The impact of Apprenticeship Carolina on employers, communities, and state tax coffers has been incredible. Imagine for a minute the effect of thousands of skilled workers on local business productivity and profitability. Think about the volume of income and sales taxes they kick into South Carolina's budget every year. People would probably look more favorably on the role of its government in industry if every one of its programs produced the positive payback that AC has generated since its inception.

It is important and exciting to note that the apprenticeships generated in South Carolina are not just in the traditional trades of carpentry, plumbing, masonry, and construction, but in the future-facing and increasingly well-paying industries of health care, information technology, transportation and logistics, and advanced manufacturing technology.

For example, Computer Sciences Corporation joined the program in 2009, opening fifty-five apprentice slots to train people in the UNIX operating system and Oracle software development. And in 2001, Biowatch Medical, which designs and manufactures real-time, wireless ambulatory patient heart monitors, created the state's first federally recognized apprenticeship program for cardiac care technicians, an eighteen-month program that involves 218 hours of job-related education through classroom, labs, and self-paced online learning. CVS, the giant drugstore chain, has also joined the program, as has General Electric, Duke Energy, Johnson Controls, 3M, Michelin, Caterpillar, and several other multinational firms. And the list continues to grow.

Pickens County, one of several locales where Apprenticeship Carolina, employers, schools, economic developers, and Tri-County Technical College have developed a coordinated campaign to start students on a path to success that runs from kindergarten through to secondary school, provides a particularly instructive model of the power of collaboration among community, educators, and industry. The county's schools focus on critical thinking skills and technical know-how from kindergarten on up, and the result is students who graduate high school with expertise in robotics, mechatronics, and many other vocational tracks. The district's schools are also closely allied with local businesses that sponsor school-to-work programs that equip students with real-life work experience.

To a third-party observer, the positive impact of all this on communities is truly palpable. I began my visit to Greenville, just minutes west of Pickens County, as a tourist and found it to be a vibrant midsize city with a revitalized downtown filled with art, music, a beautiful river park, and some fabulous restaurants. After sampling some of the local dishes (such as shrimp and grits, and a crab soup I must try to make at home sometime soon), I drove the thirty minutes to Pickens County, where I hoped to learn more about the secrets to their success.

Pickens County is a bucolic landscape of woodlots, rolling meadows, and small towns, all within sight of the Blue Ridge Mountains. It is part of rural Appalachia, historically one of America's less affluent regions, where the shutting down of cotton mills and textile plants had left many people's employment prospects low. But if the individuals I encountered during my visit are any indication, expectations for a better future are running high. A lot of that has to do with the fact that, thanks to educational reforms and close collaboration between schools, economic developers, and local employers, the county is confidently preparing its young people for stable and secure careers.

Over the course of my meetings, I learned that the county's present educational reforms have grown out of previously ineffective efforts to attract new employers to the area. Prior to the 2000s, the state and local economic development agencies had been trying to entice manufacturers and other businesses using the standard package of inducements and were getting the usual mediocre results. Then, Ray Farley, the county's director of economic development, had an insight. "Wherever we went to speak to potential employers—to Europe, Toronto, LA, Boston—we'd hear the same complaint: They all had too few skilled workers." In other words, Farley and his colleagues realized that skilled labor was a priority issue to prospective employers—equally if not more important than the tax breaks, favorable government regulation, and infrastructure that the previous incentives had been designed around. While these incentives still exist as part of the package, it was clear to Farley and others that without the added enticement of a skilled workforce, they'd have little or no relevance.

So Farley reached out to members of the local business community, school principals, and other administrators and implored them to work together to produce the skilled, quality graduates that local and prospective employers would compete among themselves to hire.

Their skill-building campaign began in the county's grammar schools, where hands-on activities in basic science, technology, problem solving, and math concepts were added to the fifth-grade curriculum. In 2011 the district opened the Pickens County Career and Technical Center, a state-of-the-art technical high school where students are taught by instructors with real industry experience and are given access to the machine tools, computers, robotic systems, and other equipment they would encounter in modern work sites. In short, the future workers of Pickens County are taught to solve problems with their minds *and* with their hands.

Today, the center offers a full-fledged Scholar Technician program that trains students in skills such as industrial electronics, robotics, and machine tool technology. The coveted spots in this program are by application only; students with poor grades, bad attitudes, and discipline and attendance problems need not apply. And, indeed, the competition gets fiercer every year, according to CTC director Ken Hitchcock, as mechatronics, machine tool technology, computer networking, and other disciplines associated with high-tech manufacturing are attracting more and more students. For graduates of the program who want even more, nearby Tri-County Technical College offers a long menu of occupational associate degree programs, many of which provide stepping-stones to four-year university degrees at schools such as nearby Clemson University.

Dick Luecke, a member of my research team who joined me on this expedition, was quick to note that the "mind and hand" underpinnings of the Scholar Technician program echoed that of the country's most sophisticated and prestigious educational institutions. "Nick, this is what places like the MIT are all about," he told me, "and they seem to be following that general model here." During a break between meetings, we looked up the Massachusetts Institute of Technology logo. Sure enough, the institute's symbol featured two men, one standing on either side of the lamp of knowledge. One was clearly an artisan, dressed in a leather apron with a hammer and anvil; the other, in the garb of a medieval scholar, was engrossed in his book. *Mens et manus*—mind and hand. The Scholar Technician. What is that saying about a picture being worth a thousand words?

Logo of the Massachusetts Institute of Technology

Tangible evidence of the success of the Pickens County system can be seen in the many awards that both grammar school and high school students routinely pick up in national and international competitions. In 2012, a team of Pickens County students took the top three places against ten other counties in the region in an engineering and robotics competition—then went on to take first place in the international championship in Detroit. In that same year, the local high school mechatronics team won the state championship and went on to be ranked third in the nation. "That told us that we were on the right track, and encouraged our community to double down," said Ray Farley.

By 2013, the county school district had the educational infrastructure it needed to offer top-quality skill-building programs to any young person who wanted them. These programs turned out to be powerful incentives in luring employers, who now flock to Pickens looking to recruit Scholar Technicians to coveted jobs in their organizations. And these employers aren't just hiring; they're actually investing in these hires' education and skill development.

"These companies . . . talk with our tenth graders—the way major league sports teams scout for talent," said Farley. "For example, people from large international companies came out here and sat down with every one of our machine tool students. They told those students, in effect: 'If you continue in your specialty area and graduate, we'll pay for you to continue your studies at Tri-County Technical College. We'll pick up your tuition costs and pay you to study and to work for us twenty hours per week. And when you've finished that two-year program, we'll guarantee you a job worth between $40,000 and $60,000 a year.' That's the level to which the competition for skilled labor had gotten to around here."

Farley and school administrators are now aiming to increase the volume and velocity of students moving through the system and into the workplace. By their estimate, the local employment market can absorb twice as many skilled workers as the school system is currently turning out. There's real demand, and they are determined to meet it.

Their biggest obstacle is the all-too-familiar "college for everyone" mindset. "Even though the percentage of college-educated households in Pickens County is below the national average, many parents still have bought in to the notion that college is the only pathway to a successful and rewarding work life," Farley told me. "That's an inaccurate and old perception we are trying to overcome."

Perhaps that attitude is not surprising in an area where vocational employment has historically meant low-paying, physically demanding, and often dangerous work in the noisy, hot textile mills that once were the only employers in the region. Even after explaining how much has changed since those days, I still heard a similar refrain uttered by parents: "That's great, but I still want my son/daughter to go to college."

But the support of the local businesses couldn't be stronger for the new programs. As former district superintendent Dr. Kelly Pew put it, "We want businesses in our community to tell us what we were doing well and where we needed to improve. We have to understand the expectations of our graduates and whether we are meeting them." And they are putting their money where their mouth is. Today the school district has a powerful Business Education Alliance, in which business leaders and managers sit on committees alongside teachers, guidance counselors, and Superintendent Pew herself. Their meetings, said Pew, give educators opportunities to learn what local businesses expect from graduates in terms of math, reading, problem-solving ability, and other workplace skills. And what they learn has encouraged teachers to change the way they educate young people and to intensify science, technology, engineering, and math education at both elementary and high school levels. "Today," Pew told me, "everything we do relates back to science and math and their application. Our kids need to think more deeply, conceptualize, and figure out how to make things work." That's the direction in which the district is pushing them today.

Allied companies have contributed to that effort. One of the district's most dedicated employer partners is United Tool and Mold, a manufacturing firm and service provider to the plastic injection molding industry. Its most active champion of Pickens County's skilling-up initiative is Jeromy Arnett, UTM's production administration manager and coordinator of apprenticeships, who has established a pilot program through which his company brings on board two high school students as junior apprentices each year. Though the program is still in its infancy, UTM already employs seventeen of that program's graduates; one has become a plant manager, and another has advanced to the level of chief operating officer.

UTM and other companies view their support of the Business-Education Alliance not as charity or philanthropy but as an investment in their own future. For UTM, the new apprenticeship program addresses two of the company's key human resources concerns. First, like in many hands-on industries, many of UTM's most skilled employees are approaching retirement; to continue to stay in business, the company needs people to fill their shoes. Second, the majority of the company's skilled workers lack the computer and programming skills that are of growing importance for the future of the company—and that CTC high school's young people already have in spades.

A regular influx of young apprentices, in Arnett's thinking, will address both these problems in concert. And, indeed, the junior apprenticeship initiative is providing a steady influx of the technical know-how the company needs, while also providing learning and mentoring opportunities for all; upon graduation, the first student apprentices recruited by Arnett in 2013 will join the company's adult apprentices, splitting their time between work in the plant and studies at nearby Tri-County

Technical College. If all goes according to plan, Arnett's young recruits will earn associate degrees from Tri-County and complete their apprenticeships at roughly the same time—triggering sizable wage hikes. "The opportunities available to these kids are immense if they develop a skilled trade and build on it," Arnett said. "And they are our future."

Which brings me to the final ingredient in the county's success formula: the strong tie with nearby Tri-County Technical College, a two-year community college. With the goal of providing a seamless transition between the region's K–12 institution and Tri-County, Superintendent Pew and Tri-County president Dr. Ronnie L. Booth worked out a partnership that allows students to take courses at Tri-County, earning dual credits and skill certifications while still in high school. In addition, Tri-County instructors will soon begin teaching manufacturing courses for the district's high school students, and the CTC's facilities will be used in the evening to teach Tri-County's mechatronics courses.

There Is No One Leader

Whenever I see a successful skilling-up partnership like this, I can't help but ask around for the person who put it all together. It is telling that no one I met in Pickens County, however, would credit a single person for the county's progress. Instead, all agree that it was only through the *partnership* of many talented and committed people that these programs have thrived. My own observations certainly bear that out. It's thanks to these partnerships that the industrial electronics program at Tri-County has doubled in size in just eighteen months; that the mechatronics and welding programs at CTC and Tri-County have grown substantially; that parents are now beginning to talk about Tri-County Technical College as a career avenue for their children; and that recruiters and prospective employers are visiting Pickens County in droves.

"I think this is working because no one imposed a complicated structure on us," said Ray Farley. "We simply had mature people who saw the problem and jumped on it, with no personal agendas getting in the way." To those ingredients for success I'd also add trust, openness to new ideas, and a real hope and vision for the long-term future of its region and its people. All of which made me wonder: How can we replicate this kind of thinking to achieve the things Pickens County achieves across the United States? Across the globe?

The answer is that only when governments, countries, states, communities, schools, and businesses start working together with the same spirit and camaraderie I witnessed in Pickens County can we change the status quo in education and skills training in a powerful and substantial way. Until then, instances of innovation will continue to be too few and far between—producing a dozen skilled people here each year, a few dozen there—but in numbers far too small to close the ever-widening middle-skills gap and ensure a better future for the next generation. Thus the charge before policy makers, government, educators, executives, and parents is to embrace the core elements described in this chapter—and pass the recipe around.

I propose we start a movement—a movement to create a world where a practical, skills-based pathway to gainful, secure, and well-paying employment is a viable and available option for every American who wants to choose, change, or travel the skills-based career path. My research has convinced me without a shadow of a doubt that if we commit to working together, the way they have in Pickens County, we *can* make this vision a reality. So let's get started. The time to act is now.

PROGRAM HIGHLIGHT: WORKING TOWARD A COMMON GOAL

To me the most striking feature of the Pickens County story is the strong alliance and collaboration its school district has developed with economic development groups and area employers. These initiatives are deeply embedded in the culture of the community. The community believes that mind and hand are the keys to success and, most important, all involved are pulling in the same direction.

Conclusion

Thus far, we've read a lot of inspiring success stories of people who found their way to rewarding and lucrative professional futures through meaningful skills-based work. We've visited a number of thriving, productive workplaces where companies are securing their own economic futures by hiring and building skilled workforces. We've looked at facts, figures, and cold, hard economic data that debunk the assumption that a traditional classroom or lecture hall is the best or only place to learn. And we've examined research that has hopefully proven beyond a shadow of a doubt that vocational and technical educational paths can lead to meaningful, upwardly mobile, and well-paying careers.

Together we have identified many educational and economic opportunities the skills gap is creating for businesses big and small, and workers young and old. We have seen how the models of collaboration between companies, schools, unions, and governments can lead to a more healthy equilibrium between the supply and demand of skilled people in the workforce, to the benefit of individual workers, companies, and economies at large. And, finally, we've looked at research showing that closing the middle-skills gap and ending the shortage of skilled workers across a range of industries and businesses is an economic imperative for the United States as well as other countries around the globe.

Our visit to the Siemens Charlotte Energy Hub plant in North Carolina, for example, showcased a sterling example of how companies can ensure an ample supply of skilled hands through a multi-pronged strategy that includes collaborations with high schools and community/technical colleges, homegrown apprenticeship programs, and a commitment to the continuing and ongoing education of its current and future employees. The Energy Hub plant has its eye on the talent it will need in its future workforce, and is working to systematically build that talent, several layers at a time.

What these examples show is that we are at the dawn of a new era that will provide a far broader range of educational and employment opportunities than ever before— ones that can narrow the skills gap and make our local, national, and global economies stronger. The conversation around careers is changing; the mindset that college is the best or only route to professional and financial success is slowly unraveling, and the stigma against vocational and skills-based training is finally starting to dissolve.

The skills-based revolution has well and truly begun.

As I was putting the final touches on this chapter back in late January 2014, I half-overheard on my office radio a news report on a trip by President Barack Obama to a General Electric heavy equipment manufacturing plant in Waukesha, Wisconsin, near Milwaukee. I sat back and listened.

During his visit, the announcer reported, the president ordered a full-scale review federal training programs—the goal being to determine which programs worked best, and then double down on those. On that same visit, Obama announced $500 million in grants to bolster community colleges–employer partnerships aimed at training people for high-demand jobs—precisely like the ones we observed in Pickens County and Charlotte, and what German companies have been doing so well and for so long. Even more encouraging, in his speech the president acknowledged that many of the high-paying jobs of the future will go to those who did *not* attend a traditional four-year college. "Some of those jobs," he told his audience, "pay more than what you can earn with a college degree."

At its heart, though, this isn't about politics or policy or even economics. It's about the people—people like you and me—whose lives have been transformed by all that a skills-based career has to offer. So if you come away with anything from the inspiring stories in these pages, I hope it's the understanding that long-term professional, educational, and personal success does not need to be measured by the pedigree of the school you attended, the type of academic degree you acquire, or the nature of the work that you choose to do. No matter your aspirations, or the specific pathway you choose, I believe there is a certain recipe for successful career and life planning—a secret sauce, if you will—for achieving all your dreams and goals.

The Secret Sauce

That recipe starts by focusing on, choosing, and being comfortable with pursuing the educational and employment path meant for you—be it skills-based and technical, or in the arts and sciences. Always lead with your passion, and bring the highest work ethic and standards to the opportunities you pursue and the career decisions you make. In skills-based careers, just as in any other worthwhile endeavor, there is a direct correlation between the effort you put in and the rewards you get out. The mastery of the technical, in other words, is not enough; true success requires an ongoing curiosity, drive, and thirst for knowledge. So no matter what path you choose, be ready to embrace new learning experiences, meet the challenges and demands placed on you, and continuously look for ways to grow and improve. And do not forget that the ability to ask for help or guidance is critical in getting you to where you want to go.

This recipe holds true for the young adult trying to decide how best to launch her career; the midcareer worker who finds himself needing to upgrade or replace skills with new ones because of shifts in his industry, technological change, or competition from new sources; the mature professional who instead of retiring intends to stay engaged and productive in the workforce; or truly anyone at any age or stage in their professional journey with a desire to pursue their dreams and make a difference in the world.

The Last Word: There's More Than One Way to Make Chicken Stock

In the prologue I mentioned the chicken stock I prepared with loving care in the first weeks on my vocational journey as a young apprentice. Well, there is actually a little more to that story (and how it impacted my perspective) that I'd like to share. I first learned how to make chicken stock under the watchful tutelage of an Austrian chef named Johann. This stock was an important base ingredient for the hotel's famous Swan River crayfish and poached avocados in saffron butter dish. (Here, "crayfish" refers to a spiny lobster—like a Maine lobster with just a few more spikes.) That night, eager to show off my newfound skills, I rushed home and made some of that very stock for my parents. By this time, my father was coming to terms with my career choice and was more than happy to sample the fruits of my labors. Being of European heritage, he put some semolina dumplings and a few carrots in the stock, and declared it delicious.

A few days later, back in the kitchen, Chef Bruce, whom you met earlier, offered me the opportunity to showcase my new skill as taught by Johann. "Mr. Wyman, make some chicken stock!" he ordered. "Yes, Chef," I dutifully replied, and followed Johann's recipe exactly, just as I had been taught. So I was more than a little surprised when Chef Bruce was less than pleased with the result.

"That's not how you make chicken stock, this is how!" he exclaimed. I couldn't figure out what had gone wrong, until the hotel's executive chef, Klaus Lemm, pulled me aside for some words of wisdom. "Nicklaus," he said in his Germanic accent, "when Johann is in charge make it his way and when Bruce is in charge make it his way. When I am in charge make it my way. When you are in charge one day, make it your way."

That was when I realized there is more than one "right" way to make chicken stock.

Of course, this story isn't really about chicken stock. The point is that there is plenty of career advice out there. I'm not here to tell you what the right advice is for you. What I am here to tell you is that when considering your next step, take in as much information and guidance as you can, but ultimately only you can make the decision about what job or career will be the right fit.

The possibilities for your future are virtually limitless. Whatever path you decide upon, I hope it's one that offers you the unparalleled sense of meaning and satisfaction that comes from skilled work.

Appendix

Wherever you are in life—whether you are approaching the school-to-work transition, reentering the workforce, or contemplating a change from one career to another—*Job U* was written to provide you with both the practical tools and the inspiration to make your work life more fulfilling and financially rewarding. Of course, no two people are the same, nor will they travel the exact same path. To that end, I have tried to present you with the broadest range of educational opportunities and options—career- and technical-focused high schools, community and technical colleges, private craft schools, other postsecondary institutions, and online learning. And at the same time, I've endeavored to introduce you to the broadest range of *people*—people of all ages, backgrounds, and hailing from all corners of the country—who seized these opportunities and followed their dreams.

As a final note, I'd like to leave you with a brief summary of the skills-learning opportunities discussed in *Job U*, as well as a list of additional resources and a guide to where the best learning and earning opportunities are on offer.

CERTIFICATION PROGRAMS

As you'll recall from chapter 3, certification programs are a relatively fast and inexpensive way to build marketable workplace skills that increase employability and earning potential. The U.S. Department of Labor lists more than five thousand such programs under various general categories, by occupation and industry, on its CareerOne-Stop website: www.careeronestop.org/EducationTraining/Find/certification-finder.aspx. Certificate programs are offered through career and technical education high schools, community and technical colleges, four-year postsecondary schools, and in industry settings.

ASSOCIATE DEGREES

Want to go deeper? In chapter 4 we learned about occupationally oriented associate degrees, which can be earned at your local community or technical college and will take two years of full-time study to complete—perhaps only a year if you already have a college degree. The number of different occupations available through associate degree programs is mind-boggling.

The *Occupational Outlook Handbook* by the U.S. Bureau of Labor Statistics allows you to search occupations by the level of education, in this case associate degrees. You can find it at www.bls.gov/ooh.

Go to "Select Occupations By," then drop down "Entry-Level Education" to "Associate's Degree." You can also add other fields such as pay rates and industry projections.

APPRENTICESHIPS

In chapter 5, we learned about the power and promise of modern apprenticeships, where skills are learned through hands-on experience in the workplace under the direct supervision of a skilled expert. As you read in that chapter, today's modern apprenticeships look nothing like the image you might have in your head of the seventeenth-century artisan or craftsman; they have expanded well beyond the artisan trades and into industries ranging from engineering to information technology to sales and marketing. Here are some resources for anyone seeking to find an apprenticeship program in their chosen field.

The U.S. Department of Labor Employment Training and Administration registered apprenticeship website has useful information, including what occupations can be apprenticed, comprehensive FAQs, and a portal with information for parents. You can find it at www.doleta .gov/oa.

You may also like to pay a visit to the American Institute for Innovative Apprenticeship. The site has information on apprenticeships in many states as well as an excellent listing of apprenticeships in Germany, the

United Kingdom, Canada, Switzerland, and Australia. Go here: http://innovativeapprenticeship.org.

ONLINE OCCUPATIONAL LEARNING

Finally, we learned about how anyone at any age or stage in their career can keep their skill sets refreshed and relevant through on-the-job learning and training opportunities. Here, the menu of options available to you will depend on the policies of your specific company, but no matter where you work or what your position is, I strongly encourage you to approach your manager or HR representative and inquire about what programs and courses are available. Remember, even if your company doesn't offer any that satisfy your particular interests or learning needs, it never hurts to ask. Many companies will happily provide tuition reimbursement to ambitious employees looking to add value to the company by enhancing their skills and abilities. And even if you work for a company that won't, you can still take your skills development into your own hands and take advantage of the many (and often free or affordable) occupational online learning opportunities.

There are literally thousands of e-learning websites. What's important is to do comprehensive research to ensure that the training offered will meet your needs. Here are some MOOCs associated with leading universities:

www.edx.org
www.coursera.org
www.udacity.com

It also pays to visit the websites of reputable education providers in your community—most these days offer e-learning opportunities.

GENERAL CAREER ADVICE

Looking for more general career advice? This site lists more than nine hundred career options, grouped by industry: www.mynextmove.org. They even have a site for veterans looking for civilian careers: www.mynextmove.org/vets. It is easy to see which professions can be apprenticed. If it's something more specialized you are looking for, such as jobs in the green economy, look toward sites such as www.onetonline.org/find/green.

It is also worth visiting industry association websites, of which there are literally hundreds. For example, look at a site of the American Institute of Graphic Arts, www.aiga.org/career-advice; the Manufacturing Institute, www.themanufacturinginstitute.org; or Skills USA (formerly Vocational Industrial Clubs of America), www.skillsusa.org.

Career changers or people who may have been laid off who want to scope out new pathways should visit www.myskillsmyfuture.org.

Notes

PROLOGUE

1. Matthew B. Crawford, *Shop Class as Soulcraft* (London: Penguin, 2009), 15.

2. "Making College Pay," *New York Times,* February 12, 2014, http://www.nytimes.com/2014/02/13/opinion/making-college-pay.html?_r=0.

CHAPTER 1: PEOPLE WITHOUT JOBS AND JOBS WITHOUT PEOPLE

1. Jennifer Silva, *Coming Up Short: Working-Class Adulthood in an Age of Uncertainty* (New York: Oxford University Press, 2013), 4.

2. Rana Foroohar, "The School That Will Get You a Job," *Time,* February 13, 2014, http://time.com/#7066/the-school-that-will-get-you-a-job.

3. Deloitte Consulting LLP and the Manufacturing Institute, "The Skills Gap in Manufacturing," 2011, 3.

4. Ibid., 9, see figure 10.

5. Thomas J. Duesterberg, "Should We Rethink Our 'College for All' Culture?," *Huffington Post,* June 9, 2014, http://www.huffingtonpost.com/ thomas-j-duesterberg/should-we-rethink-our-col _b_5474390.html.

6. Foroohar, "The School That Will Get You a Job."

7. Erika Andersen, "How Google Picks New Employees (Hint: It's Not About Your Degree)," *Forbes,* April 7, 2014, http://www.forbes.com/sites/erikaan dersen/2014/04/07/how-google-picks-new-employ ees-hint-its-not-about-your-degree.

8. McKinsey and Company, "The World at Work," June 2012, 2.

CHAPTER 2: UNSKILLING A NATION

1. Robert I. Lerman and Felix Raluner, "Apprenticeship in the United States," in *Work and Education in America: The Art of Integration,* ed. Antje Barabasch and Felix Rauner (New York: Springer Press), 2012.

2. Joe Klein, "Learning That Works," *Time,* May 14, 2012.

3. "America's Misplaced Disdain for Vocational Education," *Economist,* June 17, 2010.

4. Harvard Graduate School of Education, "Pathways to Prosperity," February 2011, 18.

5. Howard Gardner, *Frames of Mind: The Theory of Multiple Intelligences* (New York: Basic Books, 1983).

6. Kenneth Gray, "The Baccalaureate Game: Is It Right for All Teens?," *Phi Delta Kappan,* April 1996, 528.

7. Harvard Graduate School of Education, "Pathways to Prosperity," 24.

8. National Conference of State Legislatures, *Improving College Completion—Reforming Remedial Education.*

9. Kenneth Gray and Edwin Herr, *Other Ways to Win,* 3rd ed. (Thousand Oaks, CA: Corwin Press, 2006), 83.

10. A. McCormick and P. Knepper, "A Descriptive Summary of Bachelor's Degree Recipients One Year Later," NCES Publication No. 96-158, U.S. Department of Education, 1996.

11. Richard Vedder, Christopher Danhart, and Jonathan Robe, "Why Are Recent College Graduates Unemployed?," Center for College Affordability and Productivity, January 2013, 12.

12. CollegeMeasures.org. See David Koeppel, "Why College Grads Are Heading Back to Community College," *CNN Money,* November 20, 2012.

13. U.S. Department of Education, Office of Vocational and Adult Education, Carl D. Perkins Career

and Technical Education Act of 2006, Report to Congress on State Performance, Program Year 2007–8, Washington, D.C.

14. Gray and Herr, *Other Ways to Win,* 27. Based on survey data compiled by the National Center for Education Statistics.

CHAPTER 3: CAREER AND TECHNICAL HIGH SCHOOLS AND SKILL CERTIFICATIONS

1. A. Eck, "Job-Related Education and Training: Their Impact on Earnings," *Monthly Labor Review* 116, U.S. Department of Labor, October 4, 1993, 21–38.

2. Andrew Sum and Don Gillis, "The Continued Crisis in Teen Employment in the U.S. and Massachusetts," Center for Labor Market Studies, Northeastern University and the Massachusetts Workforce Association Board, March, 5, 2012, 7–8.

3. Alison Fraser, "Vocational-Technical Education in Massachusetts," Pioneer Institute White Paper no. 42, October 2008, 1.

4. Achieve Inc., "Rising to the Challenge: Are High School Graduates Prepared for College and Work?," February 2005, 6. Accessed at http://www.achieve .org/files/pollreport_0.pdf.

5. Ibid., 2.

6. Ibid.

7. Ibid., 6.

8. Ibid.

9. Ibid., 8.

CHAPTER 4: THE POWER OF ASSOCIATE DEGREES

1. Achieve Inc., "Rising to the Challenge," 8.

2. The College Board, "Average Undergraduate Charges by Sector, 2012–2013," http://trends.col legeboard.org/college-pricing/figures-tables/average -published-undergraduate-charges-sector-2012-13.

3. National Center for Education Statistics—2010.

4. Thomas J. Snyder, *The Community College Career Track* (New York: John Wiley, 2012).

CHAPTER 5: THE MAGIC OF APPRENTICESHIPS

1. UK Department of Business Innovation and Skills, "Apprenticeships Score Top Marks from Businesses and Apprentices," August 2013.

2. Ibid.

3. United States Department of Labor Employment and Training Administration, "Registered Apprenticeship National Results, Fiscal Year 2013 (10/01/2012 to 9/30/2013)," http://www.doleta .gov/oa/data_statistics.cfm.

4. Besides a high school diploma or GED, program applicants must demonstrate college-level abilities

in math and reading, be able to distinguish colors, .and pass an interview and assessment test.

CHAPTER 6: SKILLING UP

1. EdX, "Science and Cooking: From Haute Cuisine to Soft Matter Science," https://www.edx.org/course/harvardx/harvardx-spu27x-science-cooking-haute-639.

CHAPTER 7: BRIDGING THE GAP

1. National Economic & Social Rights Initiative, "Promoting Dignity in New York City Schools," http://www.nesri.org/programs/promoting-dignity-in-new-york-city-schools.

2. Gerald Chertavian, *A Year Up* (New York: Viking, 2012).

3. To see the documents associated with the Apprenticeship Carolina program, go to http://www.apprenticeshipcarolina.com/resources.html.

People Who Are Making a Difference

In writing this book, I have found, followed, and am now fulfilling a career dream. This would not have been possible without many people. Thank you to the many friends and colleagues who recognized the need for this book and freely gave their time, insights, and perspectives.

I am grateful to the dedicated research team, including Richard Luecke and Joanne Gedge. A special acknowledgment to Patti Hunt Dirlam, who provided me with some wonderful inspiration and insights from concept to publication. I would also like to acknowledge Frederick Maddern OBE for his staunch support and Stanley Litow from IBM for his great insights and inspiration.

To the many supporters of my endeavors in skilled careers: Rob Gell AM, James Lawrence, Sophie Ramsey, Chris Ingram, William Galvin OAM, Simon Home, Tony Scimonello, Anna Sannen, Larry Biscotti, Dante Disparte, and David Pascual. Your support is very much appreciated.

Thank you to the passionate people in the companies and organizations I visited: Yvette Monet, Anna Mc-Dowell, Clare Salter, Anita Gambill, Susan Livingston,

Bill Andresen, Scott Neal Wilson, Nancy Jenner, Shelly Schneider, Carla Whitlock, and Manjari Raman to name a few. Thank you to the Winston Churchill Memorial Trust, the Park Family, the Organization for Economic Co-operation and Development, the American Institute for Innovative Apprenticeship, the team at the Institute for Workplace Skills and Innovation, and Dr. Robert Lerman from the Urban Institute.

A special thank you to my wife, Prue; son, James; and daughter, Alexandra, who continues to be a wonderful junior research assistant. Thank you to my parents, Kim and Roberta. Thanks also to Talia Krohn, a passionate person and wonderful editor. I would also like to recognize all the team at Crown Business and Lynn Johnston Literary.

Last but not least, the people and companies featured in this book. Thank you for sharing your stories.

Index